100 Under 200 Calorie Desserts

Low Calorie Cakes, Sweets & Cookies

by
Beth Christian

100 Under 200 Calorie Desserts

Copyright © 2013
MadeGlobal Publishing

ISBN-13: 978-1490961347
ISBN-10: 1490961348

All rights reserved. No part of this publication may be reproduced, stored in a retrieval system, or transmitted, in any form or by any means, electronic, mechanical, photocopying, recording or otherwise, except as permitted by the UK Copyright, Designs and Patents Act 1988, without the prior permission of the publisher.

M
MadeGlobal Publishing

For more information on
MadeGlobal Publishing, visit our website:
www.madeglobal.com

Disclaimer

The recipes provided in this book are designed to aid the reader with a calorie-controlled diet, they are not a diet in themselves. This book is not intended to be a substitute for consulting with your physician and any dietary change should be discussed with your physician, particularly if you have a medical condition. Neither the publisher nor the author shall be liable or responsible for any loss, damage or adverse reaction allegedly arising from the information or recipes given in this book.

Any use of trademarks, specific products, companies or manufacturers in this book does not imply any endorsement or connection with that product or company. Alternative products exist and may be more suitable for use in your case. These are simply suggestions which were used in the making of the recipes.

While the author has made every effort to give accurate measurements, calorie counts, names of publications and website addresses, neither the author nor the publisher assumes any responsibility for errors or changes that occur after publication. The author and publisher also do not take any responsibility for third party books, websites and their content.

Contents

Introduction   1

Cakes and Cupcakes   5

1. Perfect Chocolate Cake 6
2. Brown Sugar Cake with Salted Ganache 8
3. Lemony Cream Cheese Pound Cake 10
4. Almond Cake with Raspberry Filling 12
5. Marbled Buttermilk Snack Cake 14
6. Summer Peach Upside Down Cake 16
7. Warm Banana Cake 18
8. Easy Mocha Angel Food 20
9. Apple Cinnamon Streusel Cake 22
10. Pumpkin Cake with Cream Cheese Frosting 24
11. Red Velvet Cupcakes 26
12. Deep Chocolate Cupcakes 28
13. Gingerbread Cupcakes with Lemon Glaze 30
14. Carrot and Coconut Cupcakes 32
15. Lemon Lovers' Cupcakes 34

100 Calorie Chocolate Cravers' Snacks 37

16. Chocolate Dipped Apple Wedges 38
17. Indoor S'mores Snack 40
18. No Bake Chocolate Fruit and Nut Crisps 42
19. Bittersweet Orange Chocolate Bark 44
20. Italian Chocolate Cup 46
21. Banana Nutella Canapés 47
22. Chocolate Dipped Banana Bites 48
23. Chocolate Dipped Apricots 49
24. Chocolate Ricotta Cup 50
25. Peanut Butter Truffles 51

Cookies and Bars 53

26. Chewy Chocolate Chip Cookies 54
27. Oat and Chocolate Chip Cookies 56
28. Nutty Thumbprint Cookies 58
29. Banana Oatmeal Raisin Cookies 60
30. Easy Peasy Peanut Butter Cookies 62
31. Almond Crescents with Chocolate Drizzle 64
32. Dark Chocolate Orange Kisses 66
33. Chewy Fudge Cookies 68
34. Chocolate Strawberry Brownies 70
35. Chocolate Chip Peanut Butter Brownies 72

36.	White Chocolate Blondies	74
37.	Pecan Cheesecake Bars	76
38.	Low Fat Lemon Bars	78
39.	Simple Butterscotch Bars	80
40.	Chunky Monkey Bars	82

Dessert Crepes and Blintzes   85

41.	Lemon Mousse Crepes	86
42.	Raspberry Crepes with Ice Cream	87
43.	Orange Cream Crepes	88
44.	Crunchy Yogurt and Peach Filled Crepes	90
45.	Mixed Fruit Filled Crepes	91
46.	Apple Walnut Crepes	92
47.	Pan Sautéed Pineapple Crepes	94
48.	Strawberry Sour Cream Crepes	96
49.	Chocolate Filled Crepes	98
50.	Peanut Butter Crepes with Hot Fudge Drizzle	99
51.	Banana and Chocolate Crepe Parfaits	100
52.	Sweet Cherry Blintzes	102
53.	Blueberry Cheese Blintzes	104
54.	Cinnamon Raisin Cheese Blintzes	106
55.	Goat Cheese Blintzes with Honey	108

Frozen Scoops, Pops and Ices   111

56. Pina Colada Sorbet 112
57. Dark Chocolate Sorbet............................ 114
58. Lemon Cup Italian Ice 116
59. Classic Grape Popsicles 118
60. Watermelon Kiwi Pops..........................119
61. Blueberry Acai Super Pops 120
62. Raspberry Passion Fruit Granita 122
63. Strawberry Chocolate Chip Yogurt Pops 124
64. Agave Mango Sorbet 125
65. Chocolate Pomegranate Sherbet 126
66. Butter Pecan Ice Cream...........................128
67. Double Chocolate Chip Ice Cream 130
68. Spiced Pumpkin Ice Cream 132
69. Almond Gelato 134
70. Peachy Keen Frozen Yogurt...............................136

Lightened Up Semi-Homemade Classics   139

71. "Dump" Cake Remix 140
72. The Wacky Chocolate Cake 142
73. Cake Mix Chocolate Chip Cake 144
74. Fruity Dump Cake................................146

75.	Pumpkin Pecan Dump Cake	148
76.	Poke Cake Makeover	150
77.	Pudding Poke Cake	152
78.	Boston Cream Poke Cake	154
79.	Easy Biscuit Mix Cobbler	156
80.	Summer Fruit Slump	158
81.	Classic Cake Mix Upside Down Cake	160
82.	German Chocolate Upside Down Cake	162
83.	Angel Food Lemon Icebox Cake	164
84.	Banana Split Icebox Cake	166
85.	Oreo Cookie Lover's Icebox Cake	168

Pies and Fruit Desserts   *171*

86.	Cheesecake Pie with Berry Glaze	172
87.	Creamy Key Lime Yogurt Pie	174
88.	Mixed Berry Tartlets	176
89.	Petite Pecan Pies	178
90.	Florida Cobbler	180
91.	Easy Blackberry and Peach Crisp	182
92.	Baked Berry Crisp	184
93.	Phyllo Apple Strudel	186
94.	**Phyllo Fruit Napoleons**	**188**
95.	Dessert Nachos with Chocolate Drizzle	190
96.	Better-For-You Strawberry Shortcakes	192

97.	Ginger Shortcakes with Blueberries	194
98.	Individual Orange White Chocolate Trifles	196
99.	Dressed Up Fruit Salad	198
100.	Healthy Style Fruit Ambrosia	200

Temperature and Weight Conversion Charts   *203*

Glossary and Substitutions   *205*

Introduction

Being a chocoholic and having a sweet tooth can be a real problem when you're going on a diet or just trying to cut down, because desserts and chocolate tend to be the foods that you have to say goodbye to. Well, I don't know about you, but I just can't say goodbye to my sweet treats and any diet that bans them lasts, at most, about a week!

But there's good news! You CAN build desserts, cakes and cookies into a healthy eating regime, and this recipe book helps you to do that. All 100 recipes have a calorie count of less than 200 calories per serving and favorites like chocolate cake, red velvet cupcakes, s'mores, chocolate chip cookies, brownies, ice cream, dump cake, poke cake, cheesecake and cobbler have been given a low-calorie makeover – hurray!

This recipe book was devised to go with my book "Easy Alternate Day Fasting: Fast and Feast Your Way to a New You", but it is suitable for use with any low-calorie diet or by people who just want to cut down and eat more healthily. Chef Liz Scott has done an amazing job at coming up with recipes that are easy, delicious and that satisfy that yen for something sweet.

Each recipe states how many servings it makes and the calorie count per serving, so it is easy to keep track of calories. You can also combine these recipes with the main meals from my book "100 Under 500 Calorie Meals: Healthy and Tasty Recipes" to create a main meal of 400-500 calories.

If you're interested in learning more about Alternate Day Fasting, which actually isn't fasting at all, then check out the website http://www.easyalternatedayfasting.com and my book Easy Alternate Day Fasting: Fast and Feast Your Way to a New You. It's the only healthy eating plan that I have ever stuck to and it's all because you don't have to count calories and be good all of the time – perfect.

Cakes and Cupcakes

1... Perfect Chocolate Cake

When only chocolate cake will do, this quick and easy version will surely satisfy without breaking the calorie bank.

Ingredients

- 1 cup all-purpose flour
- ½ cup unsweetened cocoa powder
- ½ tsp. baking soda
- ¼ tsp. salt
- ¼ cup unsalted butter, softened
- 1 cup granulated sugar
- 1 large egg
- 2 large egg whites
- ½ cup low-fat milk
- 2 tsp. instant espresso powder
- 1 ½ tsp. vanilla
- Confectioners' sugar for dusting

Directions

1. Preheat the oven to 350 °F. Grease and flour a 9-inch round cake pan.

2. In a large bowl whisk together the flour, cocoa, baking soda, and salt and set aside. In another bowl beat together the butter and sugar until fluffy. Beat in the egg and egg whites until well combined.

3. In a measuring cup stir together the milk, espresso and vanilla. Alternately add the dry and wet ingredients to the butter and egg mixture, beating just to combine.

4. Pour into the prepared pan and bake until the edges begin to come away and a toothpick inserted in the center comes out clean, 25 to 30 minutes. Cool on a wire rack.

5. To serve, cut into wedges and dust with confectioners' sugar.

INFORMATION

Makes 10 servings
Each serving has 192 calories

2...Brown Sugar Cake with Salted Ganache

Deep flavored brown sugar combines with dark chocolate in this decadent dessert finished with a sprinkle of sea salt.

Ingredients

- 1 ¼ cups cake flour
- 1 ½ tsp. baking powder
- ½ cup dark brown sugar, packed
- ¼ cup unsalted butter, softened
- 1 large egg
- ¾ cup evaporated skim milk
- 1 tsp. vanilla
- 2 large egg whites
- 3 tbsp. dark brown sugar
- 2 oz. dark chocolate, chopped
- 1 tbsp. unsalted butter
- 1/8 to ¼ tsp. coarse sea salt or flakes

Directions

1. Preheat the oven to 350 °F. Grease and flour a 9-inch round cake pan.

Cakes and cupcakes

2. In a small bowl whisk together the flour and baking powder. In a medium bowl beat together the brown sugar and butter until fluffy. Beat in the egg. Alternately add the flour mixture and milk to the butter and egg mixture, beating to combine. Add the vanilla.

3. In another bowl with clean beaters, beat the egg whites to stiff peaks, gradually adding the 3 tbsp. of brown sugar. Fold into the cake batter and pour into the prepared pan.

4. Baked until lightly golden and a toothpick inserted in the center comes out clean, 20 to 25 minutes. Cool on a wire rack.

5. Meanwhile combine the chocolate and butter in a microwave-safe bowl and heat in 10 second increments until the chocolate and butter has melted. Spread over the cooled cake and sprinkle with the sea salt.

INFORMATION

Makes 12 servings
Each serving has 175 calories

3... Lemony Cream Cheese Pound Cake

Hard to believe pound cake is back on the menu but this light version featuring reduced-fat cream cheese, egg whites and a zesty lemon glaze will make it a regular request.

Ingredients

- 2 cups all-purpose flour
- 2 tsp. baking powder
- ¼ tsp. salt
- 1 ¼ cups granulated sugar, divided
- 3 oz. reduced-fat cream cheese, softened
- 2 tbsp. unsalted butter, softened
- Zest of 2 lemons
- 1 large egg
- 3 large egg whites
- ½ cup reduced-fat milk
- 1/3 cup lemon juice

Directions

1. Preheat the oven to 350 °F. Grease and flour a 9-inch loaf pan.
2. In a large bowl whisk together the flour, baking powder, and salt. In another bowl beat together ¾ cup of the sugar, the cream cheese and the butter until fluffy. Beat in the zest.

Cakes and cupcakes

3. In a small bowl combine the egg and egg whites, beating slightly. Add to the cream cheese mixture and beat well to combine.

4. Alternately add the flour mixture and the milk to the cream cheese egg mixture, beating just to combine. Pour into the prepared pan and bake until a toothpick inserted in the center comes out clean, about 45 minutes. Cool in the pan for 10 minutes before transferring to a rack to cool completely.

5. Meanwhile combine the remaining ½ cup sugar with the lemon juice in a small saucepan and bring to a simmer, stirring often. Reduce heat to low and cook until thickened, about 3 minutes.

6. When cake is cooled, Place a rimmed baking sheet under the rack, poke holes about 1-inch deep in the top of the cake with a toothpick, and spoon the glaze over.

Information

Makes 12 servings
Each serving has 190 calories

4... Almond Cake with Raspberry Filling

Like a classic linzer tart in cake form, this combination of flavors is always a sure palate pleaser.

Ingredients

- ¾ cup all-purpose flour
- ½ tsp. baking powder
- ½ tsp. salt
- 2/3 cup whole almonds
- 2 tbsp. vegetable oil
- 2 tbsp. low-fat milk
- ½ tsp. vanilla
- ½ tsp. almond extract
- 4 large eggs, separated
- ¾ cup granulated sugar, divided
- 2/3 cup no-added-sugar raspberry jam
- Confectioners' sugar for dusting
- Fresh raspberries for garnish

Directions

1. Preheat the oven to 350 °F. Grease and flour two 9-inch round cake pans and line with waxed or parchment paper.
2. In a small bowl whisk together the flour, baking powder, and salt.

Cakes and cupcakes

3. In a food processor grind the almond until fine. Add the oil, milk, vanilla, and almond extract, and pulse to combine.

4. Place the egg yolks in a large bowl and add ½ cup of the sugar. Beat on high until pale in color and a ribbon forms when the beaters are lifted, about 4 minutes. Add the almond mixture and stir in. Sprinkle the flour mixture over and gently stir in.

5. In another bowl with clean beaters, beat the egg whites, gradually adding the remaining ¼ cup sugar, until stiff peaks form. Stir in 1/3 of the whites and fold in the rest to create volume and lightness. Divide between the 2 cake pans.

6. Bake until lightly golden and a toothpick inserted in the center comes out clean, about 20 minutes. Cool on racks for 10 minutes before removing from pans, peeling off paper, and cooling completely.

7. Spread the top of one layer with the raspberry jam and top with the other layer. Dust with the confectioners' sugar and decorate with the berries.

INFORMATION

Makes 12 servings
Each serving has 198 calories

5... Marbled Buttermilk Snack Cake

Easy to make and even easier to eat, this vanilla and chocolate combo will please any cake craving you might have.

Ingredients

- 6 tbsp. unsalted butter, melted
- 1 cup granulated sugar
- 1 tsp. vanilla
- 4 large egg whites
- ¾ cup low fat buttermilk
- 1 ½ cups all-purpose flour
- ½ tsp. baking soda
- ½ tsp. salt
- ¼ cup unsweetened cocoa powder

Directions

1. Preheat the oven to 350 °F. Grease and flour an 8-inch square baking pan.

2. In a medium bowl stir together the melted butter and sugar. Add the vanilla and egg whites and stir well to combine. Add the buttermilk and stir well to incorporate.

Cakes and cupcakes

3. Add the flour mixture and stir just to combine. Do not over work. Pour half the batter into the prepared pan. Add the cocoa powder to the remaining batter and whisk well until no lumps appear.

4. Drop spoonfuls of the chocolate batter over the vanilla batter and run a knife through the batter to swirl. Bake until a toothpick inserted in the center comes out clean, about 30 minutes.

5. Cool slightly before cutting.

INFORMATION

Makes 12 servings
Each serving has 191 calories

6...Summer Peach Upside Down Cake

Enjoy the sweetness of ripe peaches in this easy to prepare cake that you can enjoy with a dollop of whipped topping for just a few calories more.

Ingredients

- 1 ½ lbs. fresh ripe peaches, peeled, pitted, and sliced (about 3 cups)
- 1 tbsp. granulated sugar
- 1 tsp. cornstarch
- 1 tsp. lemon juice
- 1 ¼ cups all-purpose flour
- 1 tsp. baking powder
- ½ tsp. baking soda
- 1/8 tsp. salt
- ¼ cup unsalted butter, softened
- 2/3 cup granulated sugar
- 1 tsp. lemon zest
- 1 tsp. vanilla
- 1 large egg, slightly beaten
- ¾ cup low-fat buttermilk

Directions

1. Preheat the oven to 350 °F. Coat a 9-inch round cake pan with cooking spray.

Cakes and cupcakes

2. In a large bowl, toss together the peaches with the tbsp. of sugar, cornstarch, and lemon juice, and evenly spread into the bottom of the prepared pan.

3. In another bowl whisk together the flour, baking powder, baking soda, and salt and set aside.

4. In a medium bowl beat together the butter and sugar until fluffy. Add the zest, vanilla, and egg, and beat until well combined.

5. Alternately add the buttermilk and flour mixture to the egg mixture beating to just combine. Pour evenly over the peaches and bake until golden and a toothpick inserted in the center comes out clean, about 45 minutes.

6. Cool on a rack for 10 minutes before inverting on to a round platter. Serve warm.

INFORMATION

Makes 10 servings
Each serving has 198 calories

7... Warm Banana Cake

Warm and gooey nuts and coconut finish off this banana cake version that's indulgent but low in fat and calories.

Ingredients

- 1 ½ cups all-purpose flour
- ½ tsp. baking powder
- ¼ tsp. baking soda
- ¼ tsp. ground nutmeg
- ½ tsp. salt
- ¾ cup granulated sugar
- 3 tbsp. vegetable oil
- 1 cup mashed ripe bananas
- 1 tsp. vanilla
- 1 large egg
- ¼ cup dark brown sugar, packed
- 1 tbsp. water
- 2 tsp. unsalted butter
- 2 tbsp. chopped almonds
- 2 tbsp. flaked coconut

Directions

1. Preheat the oven to 350 °F. Grease and flour a 9-inch round cake pan and line with waxed or parchment paper. Lightly grease paper.
2. In a large bowl whisk together the flour, baking powder, baking soda, nutmeg, and salt.

Cakes and cupcakes

3. In another bowl beat together the sugar, oil and bananas. Add the vanilla and egg and beat until well combined. Add flour mixture in 2 batches and beat just until blended.

4. Pour into the prepared pan and bake until a toothpick inserted in the center comes out clean, about 30 minutes. Cool on a rack for 10 minutes, then remove from pan and peel off paper.

5. Meanwhile in a small saucepan combine the brown sugar, water, and butter and bring to a boil. Stir well and cook for 1 minute. Remove from the heat the stir in the almonds and coconut.

6. Just before serving spread the brown sugar mixture over the top of the cake. Serve warm.

INFORMATION

    Makes 12 servings
    Each serving has 189 calories

8...Easy Mocha Angel Food

A ready-to-go cake mix lends its convenience to this light and satisfying dessert that will hit the spot after dinner without the guilt.

Ingredients

- 1 box angel food cake mix
- 1 ½ tbsp. unsweetened cocoa powder
- 1 ¼ cups cold coffee
- Light vanilla ice cream
- Reduced calorie chocolate syrup

Directions

1. Preheat the oven to 350 °F. Have ready two 8 or 9-inch nonstick loaf pans or one nonstick tube cake pan.

2. In a large bowl whisk together the cake mix and cocoa powder. Beat in the coffee until well combined and pour into the pans.

3. Bake until the cake is lightly golden, begins to crack, and a toothpick inserted in the center comes out clean, 35 to 45 minutes.

4. Cool cake in pan, tilted on its side. When completely cool, loosen with a knife around the edges and transfer to a plate.

5. To serve, use a serrated knife to cut slices, top with ¼ cup ice cream and a drizzle of chocolate syrup.

Cakes and cupcakes

INFORMATION

Makes 12 servings
Each serving has 195 calories

9...Apple Cinnamon Streusel Cake

Great to have on hand for a snack cake attack, with the delightful flavor of cinnamon and apples all baked up in a not too sweet delightful treat.

Ingredients

- 1 ½ cups all-purpose flour
- 1 cup granulated sugar
- 1 ½ tsp. baking powder
- 1 ½ tsp. ground cinnamon
- ½ tsp. salt
- 2 tbsp. unsalted butter, melted
- ¾ cup low-fat milk
- 1 large egg
- 1 tsp. vanilla
- 1 large Golden Delicious apple, peeled, cored, and diced

For topping

- 2 tbsp. all-purpose flour
- ¼ cup packed light brown sugar
- ½ tsp. ground cinnamon
- 2 tbsp. light butter, chilled and diced

Directions

1. Preheat the oven to 350 °F. Lightly coat an 8-inch square baking pan with cooking spray.

Cakes and cupcakes

2. In a large bowl whisk together the flour sugar, baking powder, cinnamon, and salt. In another bowl beat together the melted butter, milk, egg, and vanilla until well combined.

3. Add the flour mixture to the egg mixture in two batches, beating just to combine. Fold in the apples.

4. Spread into the prepared pan. In a small bowl combine the topping ingredients and work the butter into the dry ingredients with the back of a fork or your fingers until crumbly. Sprinkle over the cake batter.

5. Bake until the top is golden and a toothpick inserted in the center comes out clean, about 40 minutes. Cool for 10 to 15 minutes before serving.

Information

Makes 12 servings
Each serving has 197 calories

10...Pumpkin Cake with Cream Cheese Frosting

You'll love the aroma of spices as this delicious and moist cake is baking, topped off with an irresistible creamy frosting.

Ingredients

- 2 ¼ cups all-purpose flour
- 2 ½ tsp. baking powder
- 2 tsp. pumpkin pie spice
- ¼ tsp. salt
- ¼ cup unsalted butter, softened
- 1 cup packed light brown sugar
- 2 large eggs
- 1 tsp. vanilla
- 1 (15 oz.) can pumpkin puree

For Frosting

- 2 tbsp. light butter, softened
- 1 (8 oz.) pkg. reduced-fat cream cheese such as Neufchatel
- ½ tsp. vanilla
- 2 cups confectioners' sugar

Directions

1. Preheat the oven to 350 °F. Grease and flour a 13 x 9-inch baking pan.

Cakes and cupcakes

2. In a large bowl whisk together the flour, baking powder, spice, and salt. In another bowl beat together the butter and brown sugar until well combined. Add the eggs one at a time and beat in the vanilla. Beat in the pumpkin.

3. Add the flour mixture in 2 batches, beating just to combine. Spread the batter in the prepared pan and bake until a toothpick inserted in the center comes out clean, 20 to 30 minutes. Cool in the pan on a wire rack.

4. Meanwhile make the frosting by beating together the butter and cream cheese until creamy. Beat in the vanilla and add the sugar gradually, beating well to combine.

5. When spreading consistency is reached (you may add a bit more sugar if necessary) spread evenly over the cooled cake.

Information

Makes 24 servings
Each serving has 178 calories

11...RED VELVET CUPCAKES

Nonfat buttermilk is the secret to enjoying this lighter version of a favorite treat which will please dieters and non-dieters alike.

INGREDIENTS

- 1 ¼ cups cake flour
- 1 ½ tbsp. unsweetened cocoa powder
- ½ tsp. baking powder
- ½ tsp. baking soda
- ½ tsp. salt
- 3 tbsp. unsalted butter, softened
- ¾ cup granulated sugar
- 2 large eggs
- 2/3 cup nonfat buttermilk
- ¾ tsp. white vinegar
- ½ tsp. vanilla
- 1 tbsp. red food coloring

For Frosting

- 3 tbsp. light butter, softened
- 2 tsp. nonfat buttermilk
- 4 oz. reduced-fat cream cheese such as Neufchatel
- ½ tsp. vanilla
- 1 ¾ cup confectioners' sugar

Cakes and cupcakes

DIRECTIONS

1. Preheat the oven to 350 °F. Line 15 muffin cups with paper liners

2. In a medium bowl whisk together cake flour, cocoa, baking powder, baking soda, and salt.

3. In another bowl beat together butter and sugar until creamy. Beat in eggs one at a time and beat in buttermilk. Add flour mixture in two batches, beating until just combined. Beat in vinegar, vanilla and food coloring.

4. Distribute batter among muffin cups and bake until a toothpick inserted in the center comes out clean, about 20 minutes. Cool briefly in pan then transfer cupcakes to a wire rack to cool completely.

5. Make frosting by beating together butter, buttermilk, cream cheese, and vanilla until smooth and creamy. Add confectioners' sugar gradually, beating well. Add a bit more sugar if necessary to reach spreading consistency. Lightly spread over tops of cooled cupcakes.

INFORMATION

Makes 15 servings
Each serving has 190 calories

12...Deep Chocolate Cupcakes

Two forms of chocolate highlight these rich little cakes that are surprisingly easy to make.

Ingredients

- 1 cup all-purpose flour
- 1/3 cup unsweetened cocoa powder
- 1 tsp. baking soda
- 1/8 tsp. salt
- ¼ cup light butter, softened
- 2/3 cup granulated sugar
- 2 large eggs
- 1 tsp. vanilla
- ½ cup nonfat buttermilk
- 1/3 cup finely chopped dark chocolate
- Confectioners' sugar for dusting

Directions

1. Preheat the oven to 350 °F. Line a 12 cup muffin tin with paper liners.

2. In a medium bowl whisk together the flour, cocoa, baking soda, and salt. In another bowl beat together the butter and sugar until fluffy. Beat in the eggs one at a time and add the vanilla.

3. Alternately add the flour mixture and buttermilk to the egg mixture, beating to combine. Stir in the dark chocolate.

Cakes and cupcakes

4. Distribute batter among the 12 muffin cups and bake until the tops are springy and a toothpick inserted in the center comes out clean, 15 to 20 minutes. Cool for a few minutes in pan before transferring cupcakes to a wire rack to cool completely.

5. Dust with confectioners' sugar before serving.

INFORMATION

Makes 12 servings
Each serving has 165 calories

13…Gingerbread Cupcakes with Lemon Glaze

Rich and moist, these flavorful treats with the zing of ginger get a simple glaze to finish them off in reduced calorie style.

Ingredients

- 1 cup all-purpose flour
- ½ tsp. baking powder
- ½ tsp. baking soda
- 1 tsp. ground ginger
- ½ tsp. ground cinnamon
- ¼ tsp. salt
- 1/8 tsp. ground allspice
- ¼ cup molasses (not blackstrap)
- ½ cup low-fat buttermilk
- 3 tbsp. light butter, softened
- ½ cup packed light brown sugar
- 1 large egg

For glaze

- 1 tbsp. lemon juice
- ½ to 2/3 cup confectioners' sugar

Directions

1. Preheat the oven to 350 °F. Lightly grease and flour a 12 cup muffin tin.

Cakes and cupcakes

2. In a medium bowl whisk together the flour, baking powder, baking soda, ginger, cinnamon, salt and allspice. In a small bowl, stir together the molasses and buttermilk until well combined.

3. In another bowl beat together the butter and brown sugar until fluffy. Add the egg and beat well. Alternately, add the flour mixture and molasses mixture to the egg mixture, beating just to combine. Divide the batter between the prepared muffin cups.

4. Bake until the top is golden and a toothpick inserted in the center comes out clean, about 20 minutes. Cool in pan for 5 minutes before carefully lifting out of muffin tin and transferring to a wire rack.

5. Meanwhile whisk together the glaze ingredients until smooth and spoon a little over each cupcake just before serving.

INFORMATION

Makes 12 servings
Each serving has 150 calories.

14...Carrot and Coconut Cupcakes

This great flavor combination will satisfy your yen for rich moist cake with the benefit of low fat and added fiber.

Ingredients

- 1 cup all-purpose flour
- 1 tsp. baking powder
- ¼ tsp. baking soda
- ½ tsp. cinnamon
- Pinch of salt
- Dash of ground nutmeg
- 2/3 cup granulated sugar
- 3 tbsp. light olive oil
- ½ tsp. vanilla
- 1 large egg
- 1 cup finely shredded or grated carrot
- 1 (8 oz.) can no-sugar-added crushed pineapple, drained

For Frosting

- 1 tbsp. light butter, softened
- ¼ cup reduced-fat cream cheese such as Neufchatel
- Few drops of coconut extract
- 1 1/3 cups confectioners' sugar
- ¼ cup shredded unsweetened coconut

Directions

1. Preheat the oven to 350 °F. Line a 12 cup muffin tin with paper liners.

Cakes and cupcakes

2. In a medium bowl whisk together the flour, baking powder, baking soda, cinnamon, salt and nutmeg. In another bowl beat together the sugar, oil, vanilla and egg until well combined.

3. Beat in flour mixture and stir in carrots and pineapple. Spoon batter into muffin cups and bake until a toothpick inserted in the center comes out clean, about 20 minutes. Cool in pan for a few minutes before transferring cupcakes to a wire rack to cool completely.

4. Meanwhile make the frosting by beating together the butter, cream cheese, and extract until smooth. Gradually beat in the sugar to spreading consistency. Stir in the coconut. Spread frosting over cooled cupcakes.

INFORMATION

Makes 12 servings
Each serving has 160 calories

15...Lemon Lovers' Cupcakes

If lemon is your passion you'll adore these delicious cupcakes featuring fresh lemon juice and zest in a light and airy guise.

Ingredients

- 1 ½ cups all-purpose flour
- 2/3 cup granulated sugar
- 1 ½ tsp. baking powder
- 1/8 tsp. baking soda
- ¼ tsp. salt
- ¼ cup light butter, melted
- 1 large egg
- ½ cup low-fat buttermilk
- ½ cup low-fat milk
- 1 tsp. grated lemon zest

For Frosting

- 2 tbsp. light butter softened
- ½ cup reduced-fat cream cheese such as Neufchatel
- ½ tsp. vanilla
- Pinch of salt
- 2 tsp. lemon juice
- 1 tsp. grated lemon zest
- 1 ½ cups confectioners' sugar

Cakes and cupcakes

Directions

1. Preheat the oven to 350 °F. Line a 12 cup muffin tin with paper liners.

2. In a large bowl whisk together the flour, sugar, baking powder, baking soda, and salt. In another bowl beat together the melted butter, egg, buttermilk, milk, and lemon zest.

3. Gradually add wet ingredients to dry, beating just to combine. Distribute batter into muffin cups and bake until a toothpick inserted in the center comes out clean, about 25 minutes. Cool for a few minutes in the pan before transferring to a wire rack to cool completely.

4. Meanwhile make the frosting by beating together the butter, cream cheese, vanilla, salt, lemon juice, and lemon zest until smooth. Gradually add confectioners' sugar to reach spreading consistency. Spread on cooled cupcakes.

Information

Makes 12 servings
Each servings has 165 calories

100 Calorie
Chocolate Cravers'
Snacks

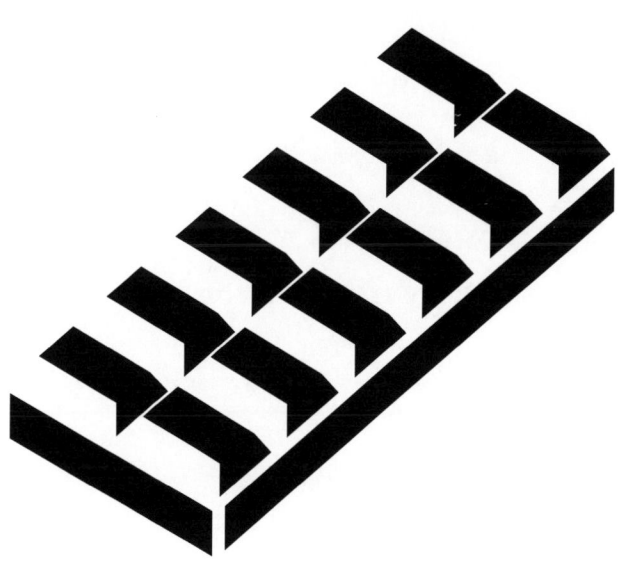

16...Chocolate Dipped Apple Wedges

For something fruity yet chocolatey, look no further than these delightful bites that are perfect for a quick snack.

Ingredients

- 1 medium apple such as Macintosh or Granny Smith
- 1 tsp. lemon juice
- ½ oz. dark chocolate, chopped
- 1 tsp. chopped peanuts

Directions

1. Halve the apple and scoop out the core. Cut into 8 equal size wedges.

2. Put the lemon juice in a shallow bowl with cold water and add the apple wedges.

3. Meanwhile melt the chocolate in the microwave at 10 second intervals, stirring with a fork.

4. Line a plate with parchment or waxed paper.

5. Remove the apples from the lemon water and pat dry with paper towels. Dip the ends of each apple wedge in the melted chocolate and place on the prepared plate.

6. Sprinkle with the chopped peanuts and refrigerate until set.

100 Calorie chocolate cravers' snacks

INFORMATION

Makes 2 servings
Each serving has 100 calories

17...Indoor S'mores Snack

No need to daydream about these treats any longer when you can have one anytime as a low calorie snack.

Ingredients

- 1 low-fat graham cracker sheet, broken into 2 squares
- 2 standard size marshmallows
- 1 (1-inch) square chocolate, melted

Directions

1. Preheat the broiler to low. Line a pan with tin foil.
2. Place the graham cracker squares side by side on the pan and top each with a marshmallow.
3. Set under the broiler, watching carefully, until the top becomes lightly browned and the marshmallow begins to melt.
4. Transfer the crackers to a serving dish and drizzle the chocolate over.

Information

Makes 2 servings
Each serving has 97 calories

100 Calorie chocolate cravers' snacks

18...No Bake Chocolate Fruit and Nut Crisps

You'll love these yummy bites of chocolate studded with sweet cherries and pistachios for an indulgent snack that can't be beat.

Ingredients

- 1 ½ cups toasted rice cereal, such as Rice Krispies
- ¾ cup dried cherries, roughly chopped
- 1/3 cup, pistachio nuts, roughly chopped
- 1 2/3 cup semi-sweet chocolate chips

Directions

1. In a large bowl stir together the cereal, cherries, and pistachios. Line a rimmed baking sheet with parchment paper.

2. In a medium glass or ceramic bowl, melt the chocolate in the microwave until soft, starting with 1 minute and then checking again at 10 second intervals.

3. Transfer the melted chocolate to the bowl with the cereal mixture and quickly stir to coat.

4. Drop by spoonfuls onto the prepared pan to make 2 dozen mounds.

5. Place in the refrigerator to set for at least 1 hour before serving.

100 Calorie chocolate cravers' snacks

INFORMATION

Makes 12 servings (2 pieces)
Each serving has 100 calories

19...Bittersweet Orange Chocolate Bark

Delicious dark chocolate and citrusy orange come together in this adult indulgence that you'll savor with every bite.

Ingredients

- 2 cups chopped bittersweet chocolate
- 1 tsp. grated orange zest
- ¼ tsp. orange oil or extract
- ¾ cup orange-scented dried cranberries, roughly chopped

Directions

1. Line a rimmed baking sheet with waxed or parchment paper.
2. Place the chocolate in a medium glass or ceramic bowl and microwave, starting with 1 minute and checking at 10 second intervals after, until soft and melted.
3. Whisk in the grated zest and orange oil and stir in the cranberries.
4. Scrape the chocolate mixture onto the prepared baking sheet and spread evenly into a ¼-inch thick patty. Place another piece of paper over the top and refrigerate until set, at least 30 minutes.

5. Invert onto a flat surface and peel off the paper. Lightly score the patty into 2 dozen squares and break the bark at the score marks.

6. Store in an airtight container.

Information

Makes 12 servings (2 pieces)
Each serving has 98 calories

20...Italian Chocolate Cup

Hard to believe this much decadence can be packed into a little espresso cup but when warm chocolate calls, here's your guiltless answer.

Ingredients

- ½ cup unsweetened cocoa powder
- ¼ cup granulated sugar
- 1 ½ tbsp. cornstarch
- 2 cups non-fat milk

Directions

1. Whisk together the cocoa, sugar, and cornstarch in a medium saucepan.
2. Add the milk and whisk while cooking over a medium heat.
3. Continue cooking at a simmer and whisking until bubbly and thickened. Remove from the heat.
4. Divide the mixture between 4 espresso cups. Serve warm or chilled.

Information

Makes 6 servings
Each serving has 95 calories

21...Banana Nutella Canapés

The great combination of chocolate and banana never fails and here the added flavor of hazelnuts from Nutella takes it over the top for an elegant snack.

Ingredients

- 1 chocolate graham cracker sheet, broken into 4 pieces
- 1 tbsp. Nutella chocolate hazelnut spread
- 4 ripe banana slices cut on the diagonal
- ½ tsp. chopped hazelnuts

Directions

1. Spread the Nutella evenly on top of each chocolate graham and place on a plate. Put a banana slice on top of each and sprinkle with the nuts. Chill for 10 minutes before serving.

Information

Makes 4 servings
Each serving has 68 calories

22...Chocolate Dipped Banana Bites

These easy-to-make frozen bites are perfect for a chocolate craving without compromising your diet success.

Ingredients

- 1 ripe medium banana, peeled
- ¼ cup semisweet chocolate chips, melted
- 1 tsp. flaked coconut

Directions

1. Line a pan with waxed or parchment.
2. Cut the banana into 9 equal-sized rounds and using a fork, dip into the melted chocolate. Immediately place in the prepared pan.
3. Sprinkle the coconut over each and freeze the bananas in the pan for 1 hour, until firm.
4. Carefully place the banana bites into a zip locked freezer bag and keep frozen until ready to serve.

Information

Makes 3 servings
Each serving has 70 calories

23...Chocolate Dipped Apricots

These are great to have on hand when something both fruity and chocolatey seems to be your goal, while good-for-you almonds add a delightful crunch.

Ingredients

- 18 dried apricots
- 3 oz. dark chocolate, melted
- ½ cup sliced almonds

Directions

1. Line a rimmed baking sheet with parchment paper.
2. Dip the apricots halfway into the chocolate and then roll in the almonds.
3. Carefully place on the prepared sheet and refrigerate until set.

Information

Makes 9 servings (2 pieces)
Each serving has 96 calories

24...Chocolate Ricotta Cup

This easy to make treat will satisfy a creamy chocolate craving in no time and goes well with fresh sliced strawberries.

Ingredients

- 2 cups part-skim ricotta cheese
- 2 tbsp. fat-free half and half
- ½ tsp. vanilla
- 5 oz. dark chocolate, melted

Directions

1. Allow the ricotta cheese to drain in a sieve over a bowl in the fridge for several hours. Discard the accumulated liquid.

2. Place the drained ricotta in a food processor and add the half and half and vanilla. Process until smooth and well combined.

3. Add melted chocolate to the processor and pulse until well combined. Transfer to a serving bowl, cover, and refrigerate for at least 1 hour.

4. To serve, spoon into a dish and add fresh fruit if desired.

Information

Makes 10 servings (¼ cup)
Each serving has 100 calories

25...Peanut Butter Truffles

Making your own truffles allows you to cut out excess fat without losing flavor, like in these sweet and salty creations dipped in chocolate.

Ingredients

- ½ cup reduced-fat peanut butter
- ¼ cup salted pretzel crumbs
- ½ cup milk or dark chocolate, melted

Directions

1. In a small bowl stir together the peanut butter and pretzel crumbs until well combined. Place in the freezer until firm, about 20 minutes.

2. Line a rimmed baking sheet with parchment paper. Using a melon baller dipped in hot water, scoop out 24 teaspoon-size balls and place on the prepared pan. Return the pan to the freezer for 1 hour until the balls are quite firm and frozen.

3. Carefully dip each ball into the melted chocolate and set on a clean platter lined with parchment. Refrigerate until the chocolate has set before serving

Information

Makes 12 servings (2 truffles)
Each serving has 99 calories

Cookies and Bars

26...Chewy Chocolate Chip Cookies

Unbelievably delicious, you may need to police yourself by packaging them up in twos and keeping them frozen for future treats.

Ingredients

- 2 ¼ cups all-purpose flour
- 1 tsp. baking soda
- ¼ tsp. salt
- ½ cup (1 stick) unsalted butter, softened
- ¾ cup granulated sugar
- 1 cup packed light brown sugar
- 1 tsp. vanilla
- 2 large egg whites
- 1 cup dark chocolate chips

Directions

1. Preheat the oven to 350 °F.

2. In a large bowl whisk together the flour, baking soda, and salt. In another bowl beat together the butter and both sugars until fluffy. Beat in the vanilla and egg whites.

3. Add the flour in 2 batches, beating well to combine. Stir in the chocolate chips.

Cookies and bars

4. Drop by the tablespoonful on a baking sheet lined with parchment paper. Bake until just lightly browned but still soft in the middle, about 8 minutes. Cool on the baking sheet for a few minutes before transferring cookies to a wire rack to cool completely. Repeat with remaining cookie dough.

Information

Makes 20 servings (2 cookies)
Each serving has 190 calories

27...Oat and Chocolate Chip Cookies

Ground oats add healthy fiber while yogurt is the secret ingredient for tenderness in these scrumptious drop cookies you can enjoy with a scoop of low-fat ice cream or frozen yogurt.

Ingredients

- ½ cup rolled oats, ground fine in a processor
- 1 ¼ cups all-purpose flour
- ½ tsp. baking soda
- Pinch of salt
- ¼ cup unsalted butter, softened
- ½ cup packed light brown sugar
- ½ cup plain low-fat yogurt
- 1 large egg
- ½ tsp. vanilla
- 1 cup mini chocolate chips

Directions

1. Preheat the oven to 375 °F.

2. In a large bowl whisk together the ground oats, flour, baking soda, and salt. In another bowl beat the butter and sugar together until fluffy. Beat in the yogurt, egg, and vanilla until well combined.

3. Add the flour mixture in two batches, beating to combine. Stir in the chocolate chips.

4. Drop by heaping teaspoonfuls onto an ungreased cookie sheet and bake until just beginning to brown around the edges, about 10 minutes. Transfer cookies to a wire rack to cool.

INFORMATION

Makes 30 servings (1 cookie)
Each serving has 80 calories

28...Nutty Thumbprint Cookies

Chewy and satisfying with roasted peanuts and oats, you'll enjoy these treats topped with a sweet dab of preserves of your own choice.

Ingredients

- ½ cup all-purpose flour
- ½ cup whole wheat flour
- ½ tsp. baking powder
- ¼ tsp. ground cinnamon
- 1/8 tsp. baking soda
- ¼ cup unsalted butter, softened
- ¼ cup granulated sugar
- ¼ cup packed light brown sugar
- ½ tsp. vanilla
- 2 large egg whites
- 1 cup quick-cooking oats
- ¾ cup chopped lightly salted roasted peanuts
- ¼ cup reduced-sugar preserves such as strawberry or apricot

Directions

1. Preheat the oven to 375 °F. Line a baking sheet with parchment paper.

Cookies and bars

2. In a medium bowl whisk together the flours, baking powder, cinnamon, and baking soda. In another bowl beat together the butter and sugars until fluffy. Beat in the vanilla and egg whites until well combined. Add the flour mixture in two batches mixing well. Stir in the oats.

3. Place the nuts in a shallow bowl. Roll the cookie dough into balls slightly less than 1-inch wide. Roll in the peanuts and place on the cookie sheet about 2-inches apart. Use your thumb to make an indent in the middle of each.

4. Bake until the cookies are golden on the edges and puffy, about 8 minutes. Transfer to a wire rack to cool. Spoon a small amount of the preserves in the center of each cookie and serve.

INFORMATION

Makes 12 servings (3 cookies)
Each serving has 180 calories

29...Banana Oatmeal Raisin Cookies

This great combo guarantees moistness without the fat, while a hint of peanut butter and honey add another layer of sweet flavor.

Ingredients

- 1 cup quick cooking oats
- ½ cup whole wheat flour
- ¼ cup nonfat dry milk
- 1 tsp. ground cinnamon
- ¼ tsp. baking soda
- ½ cup reduced fat peanut butter
- ½ cup honey
- ½ cup mashed ripe banana (about 1)
- 1 tsp. vanilla
- ½ cup golden raisins

Directions

1. Preheat the oven to 350 °F. Line cookie sheets with parchment paper.
2. In a medium bowl whisk together the oats, flour, dry milk, cinnamon, and baking soda. In another bowl beat together the peanut butter, honey, banana, and vanilla until smooth. Add the flour mixture to the banana mixture in two batches, beating well. Stir in the raisins.

3. Drop by heaping tablespoons on the cookie sheets about 2 inches apart, slightly flattening the tops. Bake until lightly golden, between 10 and 12 minutes. Cool for 2 minutes before transferring to a wire rack to cool completely.

Information

Makes 10 servings (2 cookies)
Each serving has 200 calories

30...Easy Peasy Peanut Butter Cookies

Only 3 ingredients required for these amazing cookies that anyone can mix, bake, and eat in no time!

Ingredients

- 1 cup reduced fat peanut butter
- 1 cup granulated sugar
- 1 large egg

Directions

1. Preheat the oven to 375 °F. Lightly grease a cookie sheet with cooking spray.

2. In a large bowl beat together the ingredients until smooth and well combined. Form 1-inch sized balls, roll in a little extra table sugar, and place about 2 inches apart on the cookie sheet.

3. Flatten with the back of a fork or bottom of a glass. Bake until edges begin to brown, about 8 minutes. Cool on cookie sheet for 2 minutes before transferring to a wire rack to cool completely.

Information

Makes 12 servings (3 cookies)
Each serving has 180 calories

Cookies and bars

31... Almond Crescents with Chocolate Drizzle

Ground almonds are featured in these flavorful cookies topped off with a delightful drizzle white and dark chocolate.

Ingredients

- 2 ¼ cups whole almonds, ground fine
- ¾ cup granulated sugar
- 2 large egg whites
- 1 tsp. almond extract
- 1 oz. white chocolate, melted
- 1 oz. dark chocolate, melted

Directions

1. Preheat the oven to 350 °F. Line cookie sheets with parchment paper.

2. In a food processor fitted with a steel blade place the almonds, sugar, egg whites, and extract and pulse until well combined.

3. Shape heaping teaspoons of the dough into crescents and place about 1 inch apart on the prepared cookie sheets. Bake until the edges just begin to brown, 10 to 12 minutes. Carefully transfer to a wire rack to cool completely.

4. Decoratively drizzle the melted chocolates over the cookies and allow to set.

INFORMATION

Makes 16 servings (2 cookies)
Each serving has 160 calories

32... Dark Chocolate Orange Kisses

This natural flavor pair makes for a delightfully rich and satisfying cookie treat that you'll look forward to as an after dinner treat.

Ingredients

- 2 cups all-purpose flour
- 1 tsp. baking powder
- Pinch salt
- ¼ cup unsalted butter, softened
- ½ cup reduced-fat spread such as Earth Balance for baking
- 2/3 cup granulated sugar
- 1 large egg white
- 2 tsp. grated orange zest
- 40 dark chocolate kisses, unwrapped

Directions

1. Preheat oven to 350 °F.
2. In a large bowl whisk together flour, baking powder and salt. In another bowl beat together butter, spread, and sugar until well combined. Beat in egg white and orange zest. Add flour in two batches and beat well to combine. Chill dough for 30 minutes.

Cookies and bars

3. Shape cookie dough into 1 inch balls and place about 2 inches apart on ungreased cookie sheets. Bakes until edges begin to brown, about 8 minutes.

4. Press a chocolate kiss into the middle of each warm cookie and allow to set for 2 minutes. Transfer cookies to a wire rack to cool completely.

INFORMATION

Makes 20 servings (2 cookies)
Each serving has 165 calories

33...Chewy Fudge Cookies

Intense cocoa powder flavors these easy-to-make cookies featuring the versatility of low-fat yogurt.

Ingredients

- 1 cup all-purpose flour
- ½ cup unsweetened cocoa powder
- ½ tsp. baking soda
- 1/8 tsp. salt
- 1/3 cup unsalted butter, softened
- 2/3 cup granulated sugar
- 1/3 cup packed light brown sugar
- 1/3 cup plain low-fat yogurt
- 1 tsp. vanilla

Directions

1. Preheat the oven to 350 °F. Lightly coat cookie sheets with cooking spray.

2. In a medium bowl whisk together the flour, cocoa, baking soda, and salt. In another bowl beat together the butter with the sugars until fluffy. Add the yogurt and vanilla and beat until smooth. Add the flour mixture in two batches, beating well each time.

3. Drop by tablespoonfuls onto the prepared cookie sheets and bake until set, 8 to 10 minutes. Cool briefly on pan before transferring to a wire rack to cool completely.

Cookies and bars

INFORMATION

Makes 12 servings (2 cookies)
Each serving has 155 calories

34... Chocolate Strawberry Brownies

Top with sliced strawberries and a dollop of whipped topping for a delicious treat that's particularly good warm from the oven.

Ingredients

- ¾ cup all-purpose flour
- ¾ cup unsweetened cocoa powder
- 1 tsp. baking powder
- ½ tsp. salt
- 1/3 cup unsalted butter, softened
- 1 cup granulated sugar
- 1 large egg
- 1 large egg white
- 1/3 cup reduced sugar strawberry jam
- 1/3 cup boiling water
- 1/3 cup mini chocolate chips

Directions

1. Preheat the oven to 350 °F. Generously grease and flour a 9-inch square nonstick baking pan.

2. In a medium bowl whisk together the flour, cocoa, baking powder, and salt. In another bowl beat together the butter and sugar until fluffy. Add the egg and egg white and beat until well combined.

Cookies and bars

3. Add the flour mixture and beat well until smooth. In a small bowl whisk together the jam and boiling water until no lumps appear. Pour into the batter and beat to combine. Stir in the chocolate chips.

4. Pour batter into the prepared pan and bake until a toothpick inserted near the middle comes out clean, about 25 minutes. Cool on a wire rack to just warm or room temperature before cutting.

Information

Makes 16 servings
Each serving has 150 calories

35...Chocolate Chip Peanut Butter Brownies

Gooey peanut butter swirls highlight this rich and delicious dessert that can be cut, wrapped and frozen into serving size squares.

Ingredients

- 1 ¼ cups all-purpose flour
- ½ cup unsweetened cocoa powder
- 1 tsp. baking powder
- ¼ cup unsalted butter, softened
- ¼ cup vegetable oil
- ¾ cup granulated sugar
- 3 large eggs
- 1 tsp. vanilla
- ¼ cup reduced fat peanut butter
- ¼ cup hot water
- ¼ cup mini chocolate chips

Directions

1. Preheat the oven to 350 °F. Generously grease and flour a 9-inch square nonstick baking pan.

2. In a medium bowl whisk together the flour, cocoa, and baking powder. In another bowl beat together the butter, oil, and sugar until well combined. Beat in the eggs one at a time and add the vanilla. Add the flour mixture in two batches and stir well to combine.

Cookies and bars

3. Pour the batter into the prepared pan and spread evenly. In a measuring cup stir together the peanut butter and water until smooth and drop dollops all over the top of the brownie batter. Take a knife and swirl through each dollop decoratively. Sprinkle the chocolate chips on top.

4. Bake until a toothpick inserted near the center in the chocolate part comes out clean, 20 to 25 minutes. Cool completely in the pan before cutting and serving.

Information

Makes 20 servings
Each serving has 150 calories

36...White Chocolate Blondies

Fans of vanilla and white chocolate will love these treats that can be topped with a dollop of reduced calorie ice cream or frozen yogurt for 200 calories.

Ingredients

- 2 cups all-purpose flour
- 2 tsp. baking powder
- ½ tsp. salt
- 6 tbsp. light butter, softened
- 1 ½ cups light brown sugar (not packed)
- 2 large egg whites
- 1/3 cup low-fat vanilla yogurt
- ½ tsp. vanilla
- 1 cup white chocolate chips

Directions

1. Preheat the oven to 350 °F. Generously grease and flour a 3 x 9-inch baking dish.

2. In a large bowl whisk together the flour, baking powder, and salt. In another bowl beat together the butter and brown sugar until well combined. Beat in the egg whites, yogurt and vanilla.

3. Add the flour mixture in 2 batches beating each time to combine. Stir in the chips.

4. Spread the batter in the prepared baking dish and bake until lightly golden and a toothpick inserted in the center comes out clean, about 20 minutes. Cool on a wire rack before cutting.

INFORMATION

> Makes 24 servings
> Each serving has 148 calories

37...Pecan Cheesecake Bars

Delicious pecans combine with oats for a crunchy base in this super creamy and flavorful bar just made for cheesecake lovers.

Ingredients

For the crust

- 2/3 cup all-purpose flour
- 2/3 cup quick cooking oats
- 3 tbsp. chopped pecans
- 3 tbsp. packed light brown sugar
- ¼ cup unsalted butter, diced

For filling

- 2 (8 oz.) pkgs reduced-fat cream cheese such as Neufchatel
- 1/3 cup granulated sugar
- 2 tsp. vanilla
- 4 large eggs
- 1/3 cup chopped pecans

Directions

1. Preheat the oven to 350 °F. Coat an 8-inch square nonstick baking pan with cooking spray.

2. Make the crust by combining all the ingredients in a food processor and pulsing until roughly chopped and sticky. Transfer to the prepared pan and flatten with your fingers to create an even crust. Bake for 10 minutes.

3. In a large bowl beat together the cream cheese, sugar, and vanilla until light and smooth. Add the eggs one at a time, beating well each time. Stir in the pecans. Spread over the crust in the baking pan and bake until set, about 30 minutes.

4. Cool on a wire rack and then cover and refrigerate overnight before cutting and serving.

Information

Makes 16 servings
Each serving has 178 calories

38...Low Fat Lemon Bars

Fewer eggs spell less fat but no less flavor in this delicious Southern favorite made here with a whole wheat flour crust.

Ingredients

For the crust

- 1 cup whole wheat flour
- ½ cup granulated sugar
- ¼ tsp. salt
- ¼ cup light butter, softened
- 1 tsp. grated lemon zest
- Confectioners' sugar for dusting

For the filling

- ¾ cup granulated sugar
- 1/3 cup fresh lemon juice
- 2 tsp. grated lemon zest
- 1 large egg
- 1 large egg yolk
- 1 tbsp. all-purpose flour

Directions

1. Preheat the oven to 350 °F. Coat an 8-inch square nonstick baking pan with cooking spray.

Cookies and bars

2. Combine the crust ingredients in a food processor and pulse until a dough comes together. Press evenly into the bottom of the prepared baking pan. Bake until set and firm, about 20 minutes.

3. Make the filling by beating together all the ingredients in the order listed until well combined and smooth. Pour over the hot crust and bake until set, about 15 to 20 minutes.

4. Cool completely on a wire rack before cutting and dusting with the confectioners' sugar.

Information

Makes 16 servings
Each serving has 135 calories

39...Simple Butterscotch Bars

If butterscotch is your delight you'll love how easy these super tasting bars are to whip up with only a handful of ingredients.

Ingredients

- 2 cups all-purpose flour
- 2 ½ cups packed light brown sugar
- 2 tsp. baking powder
- ½ tsp. salt
- 10 tbsp. unsalted butter
- 3 large eggs, slightly beaten

Directions

1. Preheat the oven to 350 °F. Coat a 13 x 9-inch baking dish with cooking spray.

2. In a large bowl whisk together the flour, sugar, baking powder, and salt.

3. Cut butter into small dice and melt in a saucepan over medium heat. Allow to continue cooking, bubbling slightly, until it begins to turn brown. Immediately transfer to a clean bowl and allow to cool for 10 minutes.

4. Pour the butter into the bowl with the flour mixture and stir to moisten. Add the eggs, stirring well to combine.

5. Spread the batter evenly into the prepared baking dish and bake until a toothpick inserted in the center comes out clean. Cool on a wire rack before slicing and serving.

INFORMATION

Makes 24 servings
Each serving has 175 calories

40...Chunky Monkey Bars

Chunky and chewy, these bars will please anyone's sweet tooth without too much calorie guilt!

Ingredients

- ½ cup dark raisins
- 2 tbsp. warmed apple juice
- 1 cup all-purpose flour
- ½ tsp. baking powder
- ½ tsp. baking soda
- ¼ tsp. salt
- ¼ cup light butter, softened
- ¾ cup packed light brown sugar
- ½ cup mashed ripe banana (about 1)
- 3 tbsp. low-fat buttermilk
- 1 tsp. vanilla
- 2 large egg whites
- 1/3 cup chopped walnuts

Directions

1. Preheat the oven to 350 °F. Coat an 8-inch square nonstick baking pan with cooking spray.
2. In a small bowl combine the raisins and apple juice and set aside. In a medium bowl whisk together the flour, baking powder, baking soda, and salt.

3. In a large bowl beat together the butter and brown sugar until fluffy. Add the banana, buttermilk, and vanilla and beat well. Add the egg whites and beat well to combine. Add the flour mixture to the banana mixture and beat just to combine. Stir in the walnuts.

4. Spread the batter in the prepared pan and bake until the top is golden and a toothpick inserted in the center comes out clean, about 30 minutes. Cool on a wire rack completely before cutting and serving.

Information

Makes 16 servings
Each serving has 140 calories

Dessert Crepes and Blintzes

41...Lemon Mousse Crepes

With only 50 calories per purchased crepe you can whip up these indulgent lemony dessert delights in no time.

Ingredients

- 3 tbsp. jarred lemon curd
- ½ tsp. grated lemon zest
- 1 cup light frozen whipped topping, thawed
- 4 ready-made French style crepes, such as Frieda's
- Confectioner's sugar for dusting (optional)

Directions

1. Combine the lemon curd and zest in a bowl and whisk well to loosen. Add a little of the whipped topping and whisk until combined. Add the remaining topping and fold in.
2. To prepare, lay crepes out on a flat surface.
3. Divide the whipped curd mixture between the 4 crepes, spooning down the middle. Fold over, dust with confectioners' sugar and serve.

Information

Makes 2 servings (2 crepes)
Each serving has 200 calories

Dessert crepes and blintzes

42...Raspberry Crepes with Ice Cream

Fresh fruit and ice cream are deliciously enrobed in a sweet crepe and drizzled with a sparkling raspberry sauce.

Ingredients

- 2 ready-made French style crepes, such as Frieda's
- ¼ cup reduced fat vanilla ice cream
- ½ cup fresh raspberries
- ¼ cup reduced-sugar raspberry jam
- 1/3 cup sparkling wine or champagne

Directions

Lay the crepes out flat on a serving dish. Place the scoop of ice cream on one side, top with half the raspberries and fold over.

Just before serving, whisk together the raspberry jam and sparkling wine and spoon over the top of each crepe.

Information

Makes 2 servings (1 crepe)
Each serving has 180 calories

43...Orange Cream Crepes

Sweet little Cara Cara or mandarins work deliciously here but blood oranges would add a nice touch when available as well.

Ingredients

- 2 Cara Cara or mandarin oranges, peeled, and segmented
- 4 tbsp. whipped cream cheese
- ¼ tsp. grated orange zest
- ¼ tsp. vanilla extract
- 4 ready-made French style crepes, such as Frieda's
- Confectioner's sugar for dusting (optional)

Directions

1. Halve each orange segment, reserving any accumulated juices and set aside. Combine the whipped cream cheese, orange juice, orange zest, and vanilla in a bowl and whisk well to combine.

2. Lay crepes out on a flat surface.

3. Divide the cream cheese mixture between the 4 crepes, spooning down the middle. Place half of the prepared oranges over the filling and loosely roll the crepes into a cylinder.

4. Dust with confectioners' sugar and sprinkle the remaining orange pieces over.

Dessert crepes and blintzes

INFORMATION

Makes 2 servings (2 crepes)
Each serving has 185 calories

44...Crunchy Yogurt and Peach Filled Crepes

Low fat granola adds a delightful texture to these healthy-filled crepes with the tangy creamy Greek yogurt.

Ingredients

- ¼ cup low fat granola, slightly crumbled
- 2/3 cup nonfat vanilla Greek style yogurt
- 2 ready-made French style crepes, such as Frieda's
- 1 ripe medium peach, pitted and diced
- Confectioners' sugar for dusting (optional)

Directions

1. In a small bowl stir together the crumbled granola and yogurt. Keep chilled.

2. When ready to serve, lay the crepes flat on serving plates and divide the yogurt mixture between the two, mounding in the middle. Scatter the peaches over each mound and carefully fold the crepe on each side like a package. Set seam side down and keep chilled.

3. Dust with confectioners' sugar just before serving.

Information

Makes 2 servings (1 crepe)
Each serving has 170 calories

Dessert crepes and blintzes

45...Mixed Fruit Filled Crepes

Any medley of fresh seasonal fruit will do deliciously in this simple presentation with the luxurious finish of whipped cream.

Ingredients

- 1 ½ cups fresh cut up fruit such as strawberries, kiwi, grapes, melon and blueberries
- 1 tsp. lemon juice
- 2 ready-made French style crepes, such as Frieda's
- 3 tbsp. heavy whipping cream
- 1 tsp. raw sugar crystals

Directions

1. Toss the fruit with the lemon juice and keep well chilled.

2. When ready to prepare, place crepes flat in shallow serving bowls. Mound half the fruit onto one side of each crepe and fold over into a half moon.

3. Divide and pour the cream around the edge and sprinkle the sugar crystals over the top.

Information

Makes 2 servings (1 crepe)
Each serving has 200 calories

46...APPLE WALNUT CREPES

Serve these warm with a dollop of light topping or ice cream for just a few calories more.

INGREDIENTS

- 1 Golden Delicious apple, peeled, cored, and roughly chopped
- 1 tbsp. packed light brown sugar
- 2 tbsp. water
- Dash ground cinnamon
- 2 ready-made French style crepes, such as Frieda's
- 2 tbsp. chopped toasted walnuts
- Confectioners' sugar for dusting (optional)

DIRECTIONS

1. In a medium saucepan combine the chopped apple, sugar, water, and cinnamon, stirring well. Bring to a simmer over medium high heat, cover; reduce the heat to low and cook, stirring often, until the apples are fork tender, about 8 minutes. Set aside in a warm place.

2. When ready to serve, heat the crepes according to package directions. Lay flat on a serving dish and spoon the apple mixture down the middle.

3. Sprinkle half the nuts over the apples and fold each crepe into a cylinder.

4. Sprinkle remaining nuts on top and dust with the confectioners' sugar.

Dessert crepes and blintzes

INFORMATION

Makes 2 servings (1 crepe)
Each serving has 150 calories

47...Pan Sautéed Pineapple Crepes

Top with a dollop of coconut-flavored yogurt for a true tropical delight that's super delicious.

Ingredients

- 2 tsp. light butter
- 1 tbsp. packed light or dark brown sugar
- 1 cup diced fresh pineapple
- ¼ cup pineapple juice
- 4 ready-made French style crepes, such as Frieda's
- 2 tsp. flaked coconut

Directions

1. In a nonstick skillet large enough to hold one crepe, melt and butter and stir in the sugar. Allow to bubble for 1 minute before adding the pineapple pieces. Stir and cook until the pineapple is heated through, about 2 minutes then transfer with a slotted spoon to a warm bowl.

2. Add the pineapple juice to the skillet, stir well, and bring to a simmer. Meanwhile fold each crepe into quarters.

3. Place the folded crepes in the skillet syrup and warm through, turning over as necessary to coat. Transfer 2 crepes to a serving dish, top with half the pineapple and sprinkle with half the coconut. Repeat for the second serving.

INFORMATION

Makes 2 servings (2 crepes)
Each serving has 200 calories

48...Strawberry Sour Cream Crepes

Sinfully delicious, you'll be craving these rich tasting crepes on a regular basis, so feel free to use frozen berries when strawberries are out of season.

Ingredients

- 2 cups sliced strawberries
- 2 tsp. granulated sugar
- 4 tbsp. light sour cream
- 2 ready-made French style crepes, such as Frieda's
- Confectioners' sugar for dusting (optional)

Directions

1. In a large bowl gently toss together the strawberries and sugar and allow to marinate for at least 1 hour in the refrigerator, occasionally stirring.

2. When ready to serve, place the crepes on a flat surface and spoon ½ of the strawberries down one side of each. Dot with half the sour cream and fold over.

3. Spoon the remaining strawberries with their accumulated juices over each crepe and finish with the remaining sour cream.

4. Dust with confectioners' sugar before serving.

Dessert crepes and blintzes

INFORMATION

Makes 2 servings (1 crepe)
Each serving has 135 calories

49... CHOCOLATE FILLED CREPES

You'll love these chocolate dessert treats that can be embellished with frozen yogurt or ice cream when extra calories allow.

INGREDIENTS

- ¼ cup semi-sweet chocolate chips
- 2 tbsp. low-fat milk
- 2 ready-made French style crepes, such as Frieda's
- Cocoa powder for dusting

DIRECTIONS

1. In a small saucepan (or in the microwave) gently heat the chocolate chips and milk together until softened. Stir well.

2. Lay each crepe on a flat surface and evenly spread the melted chocolate over each one. Roll into a loose cylinder and place on a serving dish.

3. Dust with cocoa powder just before serving.

INFORMATION

Makes 2 servings (1 crepe)
Each serving has 200 calories

Dessert crepes and blintzes

50...Peanut Butter Crepes with Hot Fudge Drizzle

This flavor combination can't be beat and is easy to make for a last minute sweet craving after dinner.

Ingredients

- 2 ready-made French style crepes, such as Frieda's
- 2 tbsp. reduced fat creamy peanut butter
- 2 tbsp. light Hot Fudge Topping, such as Smucker's, warmed

Directions

1. Heat the crepes according to package directions and place each on a serving dish.
2. While still warm, spread half the peanut butter over loosely roll up.
3. Drizzle the hot fudge over and serve immediately.

Information

Makes 2 servings (1 crepe)
Each serving has 198 calories

51...Banana and Chocolate Crepe Parfaits

This fun presentation will have you forgetting with every spoonful that both fat and calories are well reduced.

Ingredients

- 2 ready-made French crepes, such as Frieda's
- ½ banana, sliced thinly
- ¼ cup chocolate sorbet
- 2 tbsp. light whipped topping
- 1 tsp. chocolate sprinkles
- 2 maraschino cherries

Directions

1. Gently push the crepes down into a glass parfait glass or goblet creating a cup.

2. Layer half the banana slices on the bottom and top with the sorbet. Add the remaining banana pieces, and finish with the whipped topping, sprinkles, and cherries.

Information

Makes 2 servings
Each serving has 178 calories

Dessert crepes and blintzes

52...Sweet Cherry Blintzes

Less sugar but not less flavor, these delicious dessert treats will stand up anytime to classic calorie-laden versions and are great topped with a dollop of Greek style yogurt.

Ingredients

- 1 cup no-added-sugar cherry pie filling
- Dash ground cinnamon
- Dash ground nutmeg
- 2 tbsp. water
- ¼ tsp. grated lemon zest
- 4 ready-made French style crepes, such as Frieda's
- Butter flavored cooking spray
- Granulated sugar for sprinkling

Directions

1. In a small saucepan stir together the pie filling, cinnamon, nutmeg, water and lemon zest until well combined over medium heat. Allow to simmer for 2 minutes then set aside to cool completely.

2. Place the crepes on a flat surface and using a slotted spoon, divide the cherry mixture between the 4 crepes, mounding in the middle.

3. Fold the blintzes by folding over the sides and then rolling up into a package. Refrigerate until ready to serve.

Dessert crepes and blintzes

4. Generously spray a nonstick skillet with the cooking spray. Place the blintzes in the pan over medium high heat, sprinkle with the sugar and lightly brown on each side to just warm, about 4 minutes.

5. Serve 2 blintzes on each plate with the remaining liquid from the cherries drizzled over.

INFORMATION

Makes 2 servings (2 blintzes)
Each serving has 152 calories

53...Blueberry Cheese Blintzes

Crepes fill in perfectly for this delicious favorite that's lower in fat and calories than traditional blintzes but just as heavenly to eat.

Ingredients

- 2 tbsp. light blueberry preserves
- 2 tbsp. water
- ¼ tsp. grated lemon zest
- 1 cup fresh blueberries
- 4 ready-made French style crepes, such as Frieda's
- ¼ cup low-fat small curd cottage cheese
- Butter flavored cooking spray
- Granulated sugar for sprinkling

Directions

1. In a small saucepan whisk together the preserves, water and lemon zest until smooth over medium heat. Stir in the blueberries and simmer gently, stirring often, until the berries begin to pop. Remove from the heat and set aside to slightly cool.

2. Place the crepes on a flat surface and dollop 1 tbsp. of cottage cheese in the middle of each. Using a slotted spoon, top each dollop with 2 tbsp. of cooked blueberries.

Dessert crepes and blintzes

3. Fold the blintzes by folding over the sides and then rolling up into a package. Refrigerate until ready to serve.

4. Generously spray a nonstick skillet with the cooking spray. Place the blintzes in the pan over medium high heat, sprinkle with the sugar and lightly brown on each side to just warm, about 4 minutes.

5. Serve 2 blintzes on each plate with half the remaining cooked blueberries over the top.

INFORMATION

Makes 2 servings (2 blintzes)
Each serving has 186 calories

54...Cinnamon Raisin Cheese Blintzes

Sweet raisins and a good flavoring of cinnamon bring these blintzes to delicious heights while keeping calories low.

Ingredients

- ½ cup nonfat cottage cheese
- ½ cup reduced-fat cream cheese, such as Neufchatel
- 2 tsp. granulated sugar
- ½ tsp. ground cinnamon
- 2 tbsp. raisins
- 4 ready-made French style crepes, such as Frieda's
- Butter flavored cooking spray
- Cinnamon sugar for sprinkling

Directions

1. In a small bowl beat together the cottage cheese, cream cheese, sugar, and cinnamon until smooth. Stir in the raisins, cover and refrigerate for 20 minutes.

2. Place the crepes on a flat surface and divide the cheese mixture between the crepes, placing a mound in the middle of each.

3. Fold the blintzes by folding over the sides and then rolling up into a package. Refrigerate until ready to serve.

Dessert crepes and blintzes

4. Generously spray a nonstick skillet with the cooking spray. Place the blintzes in the pan over medium high heat, sprinkle with the cinnamon sugar and lightly brown on each side to just warm, about 4 minutes.

5. Serve 2 blintzes on each plate with additional cinnamon sugar on top.

Information

Makes 2 servings (2 blintzes)
Each serving has 200 calories

55...Goat Cheese Blintzes with Honey

This not-too-sweet ending for your meal is full of plenty of satisfaction with its creamy filling and delicious honey drizzle to finish it off.

Ingredients

- 3 oz. goat cheese, softened
- 1 tbsp. fat-free half and half
- 4 ready-made French style crepes, such as Frieda's
- Butter flavored cooking spray
- Granulated sugar for sprinkling
- 2 tbsp. honey

Directions

1. In a small bowl stir together the goat cheese and half and half until smooth.

2. Place the crepes on a flat surface and divide the cheese mixture between the crepes, placing a mound in the middle of each.

3. Fold the blintzes by folding over the sides and then rolling up into a package. Refrigerate until ready to serve.

Dessert crepes and blintzes

4. Generously spray a nonstick skillet with the cooking spray. Place the blintzes in the pan over medium high heat, sprinkle with the sugar and lightly brown on each side to just warm, about 4 minutes.

5. Serve 2 blintzes on each plate with the honey drizzled over.

INFORMATION

Makes 2 servings (2 blintzes)
Each serving has 198 calories

Frozen Scoops, Pops and Ices

56...Pina Colada Sorbet

The tropics beckon with this tantalizing flavorful sorbet made from fresh sweet pineapple and the fragrant and rich taste of coconut milk.

Ingredients

- 2 cups fresh pineapple chunks
- ¼ cup unsweetened flaked coconut
- 1 cup sweetened light coconut milk
- 2 tbsp. honey or light agave nectar
- 2 tsp. lemon juice

Directions

1. Combine pineapple and flaked coconut in a food processor fitted with a steel blade and process until as smooth as possible.

2. Pour half the mixture into a medium bowl and the other half into a blender. Add coconut milk, agave, and lemon juice to blender mixture and purée until smooth. Pour into bowl with unblended mixture and stir well to combine.

3. Put into an ice creamer maker and following manufacturer's instructions, freeze until smooth and creamy.

4. Transfer to an airtight container and keep frozen.

Frozen scoops, pops and ices

INFORMATION

Makes 6 servings (1/3 cup)
Each serving has 120 calories

57…Dark Chocolate Sorbet

Naturally low fat chocolate sorbet gets a partial sugar-free makeover in this richly flavored version made with intense tasting unsweetened cocoa and a bit of dark chocolate for another level of distinct decadent flavor.

Ingredients

- 1 cup unsweetened cocoa powder
- ½ cup granulated sugar
- ½ cup granulated sugar substitute (cup for cup) such as Stevia in the Raw
- 2 cups boiling water
- 1 oz. unsweetened chocolate, chopped
- Dash salt
- ½ tsp. vanilla extract

Directions

1. Whisk together cocoa powder and sugar substitute in a medium bowl.
2. Slowly pour in water, whisking constantly until smooth.
3. Whisk in chopped chocolate until melted and add salt and vanilla and set aside to cool slightly.
4. Then refrigerate mixture for at least 3 hours or until cold.
5. Pour into an ice cream maker, following manufacturer's directions, and freeze until smooth and creamy.

Frozen scoops, pops and ices

6. Transfer to an airtight container and keep frozen.

INFORMATION

Makes 6 servings (1/3 cup)
Each serving has 105 calories

58...Lemon Cup Italian Ice

Refreshing and light, traditional Italian ice can unfortunately be laden with sugar and sugar-free versions can be less than tasty but this version finds a happy medium with a combination of sugar and sweetener.

Ingredients

- 3 medium-size lemons, halved
- 2 cups water
- ½ cup granulated sugar
- 3 packets concentrated sugar substitute
- Mint sprigs for garnish

Directions

1. Juice the lemons, remove the seeds and measure out ½ cup lemon juice, setting aside rest of juice for another use.

2. Using a grapefruit spoon or teaspoon, carefully scrape out the remaining pulp from the lemons and discard. Place lemon halves cut side down on a baking sheet lined with parchment or waxed paper and freeze.

3. Bring water and sugar to a boil, remove from heat and stir in sugar substitute and reserved ½ cup lemon juice. Set aside to cool.

4. Pour lemon mixture into a 9-inch baking pan and freeze for at least 2 hours or until solid.

5. When ready to serve remove lemon halves and lemon ice from freezer and allow to stand for 10 minutes.

6. Scrape lemon ice surface with a serving spoon to create a snow-cone texture. Spoon into lemon halves, garnish with mint sprigs, and serve immediately.

Information

Makes 6 servings (1/3 cup)
Each serving has 70 calories

59... Classic Grape Popsicles

Kids love them and now you can love them too! Intense grape flavor highlights these refreshing, easy-to-make, treats the whole family will enjoy.

Ingredients

- ½ (14-oz.) packet unsweetened powdered grape drink mix
- 2 cups water
- 2 cups no-sugar-added grape juice
- ¼ cup granulated sugar
- Popsicle sticks and mold

Directions

1. Combine powdered drink mix, water, grape juice, and sugar in a large measuring cup or pitcher and stir until drink mix and sugar are dissolved.
2. Pour into popsicle molds and freeze for 1 hour.
3. Insert popsicle sticks and continue freezing 2 hours more or until solid.
4. Unmold and serve. Keep frozen.

Information

Makes 12 small popsicles
Each serving has 60 calories

Frozen scoops, pops and ices

60...Watermelon Kiwi Pops

You'll enjoy this summery flavor combination that's reduced in sugar but full of refreshment.

Ingredients

- 2 cups seeded and diced watermelon
- 4 ripe medium kiwis, peeled and diced
- ¼ cup granulated sugar
- 2 packets sugar substitute
- 1 tsp. lemon juice

Directions

1. Combine all the ingredients in a food processor and purée until smooth.
2. Force the mixture through a fine mesh sieve into a medium bowl. Press firmly on the solids to get as much juice extracted as possible. Discard the pulp.
3. Pour liquid into 8 popsicle molds and add sticks.
4. Freeze at least 4 hours or overnight before serving.

Information

Makes 8 servings
Each servings has 60 calories

61...Blueberry Acai Super Pops

Full of super nutritious antioxidants thanks to the blueberries as well as acai and a delightful healthy treat for a taste of after dinner sweetness.

Ingredients

- 4 cups fresh or frozen (no-sugar-added) blueberries
- ½ cup water
- 1 tsp. lemon juice
- ¼ cup light agave nectar
- 1 cup acai berry juice

Directions

1. Combine blueberries, water, and lemon juice in a medium saucepan and bring to a boil over medium heat. Reduce heat to low and cook for 6 to 8 minutes, stirring often, or until berries have broken down and liquefied.

2. Remove from stove top and allow to cool slightly before transferring to a blender or food processor. Purée until smooth and pour through a fine mesh strainer to collect the juice in a clean bowl. Press on berries to extract as much as possible and discard pulp.

3. Whisk in agave and acai juice and set aside to cool. Pour into popsicle molds and freeze for 1 hour. Insert popsicle sticks and continue to freeze for 2 hours or until solid.

Frozen scoops, pops and ices

4. Unmold before serving. Keep frozen.

INFORMATION

Makes 6 servings
Each serving has 87 calories

62...Raspberry Passion Fruit Granita

The unique flavor of passion fruit is featured in this delicious and refreshing granita ice that's not too sweet.

Ingredients

- 1 cup water
- 1 tsp. lemon juice
- ½ cup granulated sugar
- ½ cup passion fruit juice
- 1 cup frozen raspberries, puréed

Directions

1. Bring the water to a boil and add the lemon juice and sugar. Cook at a low simmer until the sugar has dissolved. Set aside to cool completely.

2. Stir in the juice and puréed raspberries and whisk well to combine. Pour into an 8-inch square stainless steel baking pan, and place in the freezer.

3. Every 20 minutes or so, stir the mixture with a fork until it reaches a grainy frozen consistency, about 2 hours in total.

4. Spoon into custard cups and serve.

Frozen scoops, pops and ices

INFORMATION

Makes 6 servings (1/3 cup)
Each serving has 95 calories

63...Strawberry Chocolate Chip Yogurt Pops

Tangy strawberry flavored frozen yogurt gets studded with bits of chocolate in this delicious treat that's low in calories and easy to make.

Ingredients

- 2 cups fresh or frozen strawberries
- 2 cups non-fat plain Greek yogurt
- ¼ cup granulated sugar
- ½ cup mini chocolate chips

Directions

1. Purée the strawberries in a food processor.
2. Add the yogurt and sugar and continue processing until well combined.
3. Pour the mixture into freezer pop molds and distribute the chocolate chips evenly, stirring slightly.
4. Insert sticks and freeze until firm, at least 5 hours or overnight.

Information

Makes 8 servings
Each serving has 110 calories

Frozen scoops, pops and ices

64... Agave Mango Sorbet

Only 3 ingredients and you're on your way to delicious reduced sugar sorbet where a combo of agave and water replaces the usual simple syrup.

Ingredients

- ½ cup light agave nectar
- ½ cup water
- 4 large ripe mangoes, peeled, seeded and chopped

Directions

5. In a small bowl whisk together agave and water until combined.

6. Place chopped mango in a food processor. While puréeing, slowly add in agave mixture and continue processing until smooth and pourable.

7. Freeze in an ice cream maker according to manufacturer's directions.

8. Transfer to an airtight container and keep frozen.

Information

Makes 6 servings (1/3 cup)
Each serving has 145 calories

65... Chocolate Pomegranate Sherbet

Deep rich chocolate flavor pairs up with tart pomegranate in this satisfying treat that's perfect for an elegant dessert.

Ingredients

- 8 oz. bittersweet chocolate, chopped
- 1 ½ cups water
- ½ cup no-sugar-added pomegranate juice
- ½ cup granulated sugar
- ½ tsp. vanilla
- ½ cup low-fat half and half
- ¼ cup fresh pomegranate seeds

Directions

1. Combine all ingredients except pomegranate seeds in a medium saucepan and whisk to combine.

2. Over medium heat, bring to a simmer and allow to cook, whisking constantly for 1 minute. Set aside to cool. Then cover and refrigerate overnight.

3. Freeze in an ice cream maker according to manufacturer's directions. During last 5 minutes of churning add the pomegranate seeds.

4. Transfer to an airtight container and keep frozen until ready to serve.

Frozen scoops, pops and ices

INFORMATION

Makes 10 servings
Each serving has 168 calories

66...Butter Pecan Ice Cream

Agave adds a delightful maple flavor to this creamy and rich tasting version of a popular ice cream selection that's loaded with the buttery toasted taste of crunchy pecans but far fewer calories.

Ingredients

- 2 tbsp. light butter
- ½ cup roughly chopped pecans
- 2 cups low-fat milk
- 1 cup fat-free half and half
- 2 tbsp. packed light brown sugar
- 2 tbsp. light agave nectar

Directions

1. Melt butter in a nonstick skillet over medium heat. Add pecans and cook, stirring often, until lightly toasted, about 3 minutes. Reduce heat to avoid butter burning. Set aside.

2. In a medium mixing bowl whisk together milk, half and half, sugar, and agave until well combined.

3. Stir in toasted pecans.

4. Freeze in an ice cream maker according to manufacturer's directions.

5. Transfer to an airtight container and keep frozen.

Frozen scoops, pops and ices

INFORMATION

Makes 9 servings (1/3 cup)
Each serving has 148 calories

67... Double Chocolate Chip Ice Cream

When chocolate sorbet or sherbet just won't do, this creamy version sweetened with agave and studded with dark chocolate bits to enhance every flavorful bite will definitely satisfy.

Ingredients

- ¼ cup light agave nectar
- 1 (1 oz.) square unsweetened chocolate, chopped
- 1 tbsp. granulated sugar
- 1 ½ cups fat-free half and half
- 2 ½ tbsp. unsweetened cocoa powder
- Pinch salt
- 2 large egg yolks, beaten
- ½ cup chopped bittersweet (dark) chocolate

Directions

1. In a small saucepan over medium heat, combine agave, chopped unsweetened chocolate, and sugar, stirring constantly until chocolate is melted. Pour into a large bowl and set aside.

2. Pour ¾ cup of the half and half into another small saucepan and whisk in the cocoa powder. Bring to a simmer over medium heat, whisking often to break up any clumps, and allow to bubble for 30 seconds.

3. Pour directly into the bowl with the chocolate agave mixture and stir well to combine.

4. Heat remaining half and half in the saucepan just to scalding. Have egg yolks ready in a medium bowl and slowly whisk in the hot half and half very slowly.

5. Return to the saucepan and cook over medium heat, stirring constantly about 5 minutes or until mixture thickens and coats the back of a spoon.

6. Pour the cooked egg mixture through a fine mesh strainer into the chocolate mixture and stir well to combine. Refrigerate overnight.

7. Freeze in an ice cream maker according to manufacturer's directions, adding the chopped dark chocolate during the final 5 minutes of churning. Transfer to an airtight container and keep frozen.

INFORMATION

Makes 6 servings (1/3 cup)
Each serving has 155 calories

68...Spiced Pumpkin Ice Cream

The earthy flavors of autumn come together in this amazing ice cream, fragrant with cinnamon, ginger, and nutmeg, and delectably rich in texture and taste with a hint of maple.

Ingredients

- 2 cups fat-free half and half
- ½ tsp. ground cinnamon
- ¼ tsp. ground ginger
- ¼ tsp. ground nutmeg
- 2 large egg yolks, beaten
- 2 tbsp. packed light brown sugar
- ¼ cup amber agave nectar
- ½ cup canned unsweetened pumpkin purée
- ½ tsp. vanilla extract
- ¼ tsp. maple extract

Directions

1. Combine half and half, cinnamon, ginger, and nutmeg in a medium saucepan and bring to a simmer, whisking often, over medium heat just to scalding. Set aside.

Frozen scoops, pops and ices

2. In a medium bowl whisk together egg yolks and sugar until well combined. Slowly pour warm half and half mixture into egg mixture, whisking constantly. Pour back into saucepan, stir in agave, and cook stirring constantly, over medium-low heat for about 5 minutes or until slightly thickened and able to coat the back of a spoon.

3. Remove from heat and stir in pumpkin, vanilla, and maple extract.

4. Strain through a fine mesh sieve into a clean bowl, cover and refrigerate for at least 2 hours or overnight.

5. Freeze in an ice cream maker according to manufacturer's directions. Transfer to an airtight container and keep frozen.

Information

Makes 6 servings (1/3 cup)
Each serving has 135 calories

69...Almond Gelato

Almond milk highlight this easy-to-make Italian version of ice cream with the enticing aroma of almond and just a hint of complimentary vanilla for added flavor.

Ingredients

- 1 ½ cups regular almond milk
- 1 ½ cups fat-free half and half
- ½ cup granulated sugar
- 2 tbsp. cornstarch
- 1 tsp. vanilla extract
- 1 tsp. almond extract
- 2 tbsp. finely chopped sugar glazed almonds

Directions

1. Combine milk, half and half, sugar, and cornstarch in a medium saucepan and bring to a simmer over medium heat, whisking often. Allow to bubble lightly over low heat, still whisking, for 2 minutes. Set aside.

2. When milk mixture has cooled slightly whisk in vanilla and almond extract and pour into a medium bowl. Cover and refrigerate at least 2 hours or until very cold.

3. Freeze in an ice cream maker according to manufacturer's directions, adding the chopped almonds during the final 5 minutes of churning.

4. Transfer to an airtight container and keep frozen.

Frozen scoops, pops and ices

INFORMATION

Makes 9 servings (1/3 cup)
Each serving has 95 calories

70... Peachy Keen Frozen Yogurt

Sweet juicy peaches and slightly tart yogurt are natural flavor partners, particularly in this custard-based version that's perfect for end of summer fresh peaches.

Ingredients

- ¾ cup low-fat evaporated milk
- 1 large egg yolk
- 1/3 cup granulated sugar substitute
- 1 tsp. vanilla extract
- 3 medium ripe peaches, peeled and diced
- 2 cups plain non-fat or low-fat yogurt

Directions

1. In a medium saucepan whisk together evaporated milk, egg yolk, and sugar. Cook over medium heat, whisking constantly for about 5 minutes or until mixture is slightly thickened. Do not boil.

2. Remove milk mixture from heat and stir in vanilla. Pour into a bowl and refrigerate at least 2 hours or until very cold.

3. Meanwhile combine peaches and yogurt in a medium bowl and stir well to combine.

4. Refrigerate while waiting for milk mixture to cool.

Frozen scoops, pops and ices

5. When both mixtures are chilled, stir peaches and yogurt into milk mixture, being sure to combine well without separation.

6. Freeze in an ice cream maker according to manufacturer's directions.

7. Transfer to an airtight container and keep frozen.

Information

Makes 8 servings (½ cup)
Each serving has 135 calories

Lightened Up Semi-Homemade Classics

71... "Dump" Cake Remix

Reducing the fat and opting for a sugar dusting rather than frosting makes this easiest of cakes a perfect dessert.

Ingredients

- ½ cup light butter, softened
- ¾ cup granulated sugar
- ¼ cup sugar substitute (cup for cup) such as Stevia in the Raw
- 1 large egg
- 1 large egg white
- 2 cups all-purpose flour
- 1 cup chopped raisins and nuts
- ½ tsp. baking soda
- 1 tsp. cream of tartar
- ½ tsp. ground allspice
- ½ cup cold water

Directions

1. Preheat the oven to 350 °F.

2. Grease and flour one 9-inch cake pan. Line the bottom with waxed or parchment paper.

3. In a large bowl, "dump" all the ingredients in at once and stir well until combined. Pour into the prepared pan and bake until a toothpick inserted in the center comes out clean and the top begins to lightly brown, about 30 minutes.

Lightened up semi-homemade classics

4. Cool in pan for 10 minutes, then remove, peel off paper, and set on a rack to cool completely before finishing dusting with confectioners' sugar.

INFORMATION

Makes 8 servings
Each serving has 155 calories

72... The Wacky Chocolate Cake

Inspired by dump cakes, wacky cakes are mixed up in the baking pan and this lightened up chocolate version is one you'll love to bake.

Ingredients

- 1 ½ cups all-purpose flour
- ¾ cup granulated sugar
- ¼ cup sugar substitute (cup for cup) such as Stevia in the Raw
- 2 tbsp. unsweetened cocoa powder
- ½ tsp. salt
- 1 tsp. baking soda
- ¼ cup light olive oil
- 1 tbsp. vinegar
- 1 tsp. vanilla
- 1 cup water

For frosting

- 1 ½ tbsp. light butter, softened
- ½ cup confectioners' sugar
- 1 ½ tbsp. unsweetened cocoa
- Pinch of salt
- ¼ tsp. vanilla

Directions

1. Preheat the oven to 350 °F. Have ready an 8 or 9-inch square baking pan (preferably nonstick).

Lightened up semi-homemade classics

2. Add flour, sugar, cocoa powder, salt, and baking soda in the baking pan and stir to combine.

3. Make 3 wells in the dry ingredients. Pour oil into one, vinegar into the second, and vanilla into the third. Pour the water over everything and stir with a fork until just combined.

4. Bake until springy and a toothpick inserted in the middle comes out clean, about 30 minutes. Set aside to cool.

5. Meanwhile make the frosting by beating together all the ingredients until smooth. Thin with a little water if necessary and spread on the cooled cake.

Information

Makes 12 servings
Each serving has 158 calories

73... CAKE MIX CHOCOLATE CHIP CAKE

Cake mixes are great standbys for quick desserts and can turn out surprisingly satisfying light desserts with the right ingredients. This quick pudding dump cake can be varied in as many ways as there are puddings and cake mixes.

INGREDIENTS

- 1 (5 oz.) pkg. vanilla pudding mix
- 2 ¼ cups non-fat milk
- 1 (18 oz.) box vanilla cake mix
- 1 cup semi-sweet chocolate chips

DIRECTIONS

1. Preheat the oven to 350 °F.
2. Grease a 9 x 13-inch baking pan.
3. In a medium saucepan whisk together the pudding mix and the milk. Cook over medium heat, stirring often, until thickened, according to package directions.
4. Remove pudding from heat and stir in the cake mix. Spread into the prepared pan and sprinkle the top with chocolate chips.
5. Bake until the edges begin to brown and a toothpick inserted in the middle comes out clean, 40 to 45 minutes.
6. Cool and serve from pan.

Lightened up semi-homemade classics

INFORMATION

Makes 15 servings
Each serving has 172 calories

74...Fruity Dump Cake

The cherry and pineapple combination here was probably the best known, but apple and other fruit varieties would be delicious as well.

Ingredients

- 1 (21 oz.) can no-added-sugar cherry pie filling
- 1 (15 oz.) can no-added-sugar crushed pineapple
- 1 (18 oz.) box yellow cake mix
- ½ cup chopped walnuts
- 6 tbsp. light butter, melted
- Light whipped topping for serving

Directions:

1. Preheat the oven to 350 °F.
2. Lightly butter a 9 x 13-inch glass baking dish.
3. Empty the cherry pie filling and crushed pineapple cans into the baking dish and stir to combine.
4. Sprinkle the cake mix evenly over, and top with the nuts. Drizzle the melted butter over and bake until the top is golden, the edges are bubbly, and a toothpick inserted in the cake portion comes out clean, 30 to 40 minutes.
5. Cool before serving or serve warm if desired.

Lightened up semi-homemade classics

INFORMATION

Makes 15 servings
Each serving has 188 calories

75...Pumpkin Pecan Dump Cake

This delicious fall flavored dessert can be kicked up with a spice cake mix or even a carrot cake one.

Ingredients

- 1 large can pumpkin pie filling
- 1 (8 oz.) can nonfat unsweetened evaporated milk
- 1 large egg
- 2 large egg whites
- 1 (18 oz.) box yellow cake mix
- 6 tbsp. light butter, melted
- 1/3 cup chopped pecans

Directions

1. Preheat the oven to 350 °F.
2. Lightly butter a 9 x 13-inch glass baking dish.
3. Pour the pumpkin pie filling and milk into the pan, add the eggs, and stir well with a fork to combine.
4. Sprinkle the cake mix evenly over the top and drizzle the melted butter over along with the pecans.
5. Bake until the top is golden and a toothpick inserted in the cake portion comes out clean, about 45 minutes.
6. Serve warm with whipped cream, if desired.

Lightened up semi-homemade classics

INFORMATION

Makes 18 servings
Each serving has 190 calories

76... POKE CAKE MAKEOVER

Lightening up this classic picnic favorite is easy to do with the use of sugar-free Jell-O and a reduced calorie topping.

INGREDIENTS

- 1 (18 oz.) box white cake mix
- 1 box sugar-free raspberry, strawberry, or cherry gelatin
- 1 cup boiling water
- ½ cup cold water
- 2 cups light frozen whipped topping, thawed
- Fruit to garnish (optional)

DIRECTIONS

1. Prepare the white cake mix in a 9 x 13-inch glass baking dish, according to package directions. Set aside to cool completely.

2. Using a fork or skewer, poke numerous holes all over the cake.

3. In a saucepan combine the boiling water and gelatin and stir until dissolved. Add the cold water and stir well. Carefully pour the mixture over the top of the cake, allowing it to sink into the holes. Refrigerate for at least 2 hours.

4. Spread the whipped cream or topping over the cake decoratively before serving and garnish with the fruit if using.

INFORMATION

Makes 15 servings
Each serving has 138 calories

77...Pudding Poke Cake

Gelatin and pudding mix join forces in this easy poke cake that offers additional texture and creaminess with a lot less calories.

Ingredients

- 1 (18 oz.) box white cake mix
- 1 box sugar-free lime gelatin
- 1 cup boiling water
- ½ cup cold water
- 1 box sugar-free white chocolate pudding mix
- 2 cups nonfat milk
- Fruit to garnish

Directions

1. Prepare the white cake mix in a 9 x 13-inch glass baking dish, according to package directions. Set aside to cool completely.

2. Using a fork or skewer, poke numerous holes all over the cake.

3. In a saucepan combine the boiling water and gelatin and stir until dissolved. Add the cold water and stir well. Carefully pour the mixture over the top of the cake, allowing it to sink into the holes. Refrigerate for at least 2 hours.

Lightened up semi-homemade classics

4. Meanwhile prepare the white chocolate pudding mix with the milk according to package directions and allow to cool somewhat, stirring occasionally. While still lukewarm, spread over the poke cake and continue to refrigerate until the cake and pudding are cold, another hour or more.
5. Serve garnished with fruit.

INFORMATION

Makes 15 servings
Each serving has 132 calories

78...Boston Cream Poke Cake

This great combination of vanilla and chocolate makes for a perfect poke cake and here, with its lightened up ingredients, you'll be amazed at the satisfying result.

Ingredients

- 1 (18 oz.) box yellow cake mix
- 1 box sugar-free vanilla pudding mix
- 2 cups nonfat milk
- 1 cup chopped dark chocolate
- 1/3 cup fat-free half and half, warmed

Directions

1. Prepare the yellow cake mix as directed in a 9 x 13-inch glass baking dish. Set aside to cool completely.

2. Meanwhile make the pudding with the milk according to package directions and allow to cool somewhat, stirring occasionally.

3. When the cake is cool, poke holes all over it with a skewer or fork and pour half the pudding mix over the top. Spread evenly and refrigerate. When the remaining pudding is cool, spread on top and continue to chill.

4. Prepare the chocolate topping by whisking together the chocolate pieces and warm half and half until smooth and glossy. Allow to cool to lukewarm temperature and then pour and spread evenly over the chilled pudding poke cake.

Lightened up semi-homemade classics

5. Return to the fridge to cool the cake completely. Serve chilled.

Information

Makes 18 servings
Each serving has 192 calories

79...Easy Biscuit Mix Cobbler

This cobbler "takes the cake" when it comes to easy preparation thanks to a light biscuit mix and frozen fruit.

Ingredients

- ½ cup reduced sugar strawberry jam or preserves
- ¼ cup water
- 2 tbsp. granulated sugar
- 2 cups frozen strawberries or mixed berries, thawed
- 1 tbsp. light butter, diced

For the cobbler topping

- 1 ¼ cups light biscuit mix, such as Heart Smart Bisquick®
- 2 tbsp. granulated sugar
- ¼ cup nonfat milk
- ¼ cup plain low-fat Greek style yogurt

Directions

1. Preheat the oven to 350 °F.

2. Lightly butter a 9-inch square baking dish.

3. In a medium saucepan combine the jam, water, and sugar, and heat over medium heat until sugar is dissolved, stirring often. Remove from heat and stir in strawberries. Pour into prepared pan and dot with the diced butter.

Lightened up semi-homemade classics

4. In a medium bowl stir together the cobbler topping ingredients just until combined and spoon over the strawberries.

5. Bake until the cobbler is golden, the fruit is bubbly, and a toothpick inserted in the crust comes out clean, 30 to 40 minutes.

INFORMATION

Makes 9 servings
Each serving has 179 calories

80...Summer Fruit Slump

Made completely on top of the stove, this quick dessert gets its name from the way the drop dumplings "slump" over when dished up.

Ingredients

- 4 cups fresh summer fruit such as diced plums, peaches, nectarines and berries
- 3 tbsp. packed light brown sugar
- 1/3 cup water plus 1 TB
- 2 tsp. cornstarch
- 1 cup light biscuit mix, such as Heart Smart Bisquick®

Directions

1. In a medium heavy-bottomed pot, combine the fruit with the sugar and 1/3 cup of the water. Bring to a simmer over medium heat, stir gently, cover and cook for 5 minutes. Remove from heat.

2. In a small bowl combine the remaining tbsp. of water and the cornstarch and stir into the fruit mixture. In another bowl, prepare the biscuit mix as dumplings, according to the package directions.

3. Return the fruit pot to the stove and bring to a simmer, stirring often. Reduce the heat to low, spoon 8 dumplings on top of the fruit, cover and cook on low until the dumplings are firm, about 10 minutes.

Lightened up semi-homemade classics

4. Set aside to rest for 10 minutes before spooning and serving.

INFORMATION

Makes 8 servings
Each serving has 155 calories

81...Classic Cake Mix Upside Down Cake

This simple recipe is lightened up with the use of yogurt and healthier dried cherries for a terrific take on an old classic.

Ingredients

- ¼ cup light butter
- ½ cup packed light brown sugar
- 12 no-sugar-added pineapple rings, canned or fresh
- ¼ cup dried cherries
- 1 box (18 oz.) yellow cake mix
- 1 cup nonfat plain Greek yogurt
- 1 cup water

Directions

1. Preheat the oven to 350 °F. Dice the butter and place in a 9 x 13-inch baking pan. Place in the oven briefly just to melt the butter. Sprinkle the brown sugar over evenly.

2. Place the pineapple rings decoratively on top of the butter and sugar mixture and sprinkle the dried cherries in the centers of the rings.

3. Prepare the cake mix batter using the yogurt and water instead of recommended ingredients and pour over the pineapple. Spread evenly.

Lightened up semi-homemade classics

4. Bake until the cake is lightly golden and a toothpick inserted in the center comes out clean, 40 to 45 minutes. Remove from oven and run a knife around the edges of the pan.

5. Carefully place a rimmed cookie sheet or platter over the cake and flip upside down – do not remove pan yet. After 5 to 10 minutes lift up pan and allow sugar mixture to drip over.

6. Cool slightly before serving.

INFORMATION

Makes 12 servings
Each serving has 190 calories

82...German Chocolate Upside Down Cake

You'll love this pseudo "upside down" version made with cake mix and reduced fat ingredients.

Ingredients

- ½ cup chopped pecans
- 2/3 cup unsweetened flaked coconut
- 1 box (18 oz.) German chocolate cake mix
- 1 cup nonfat plain Greek yogurt
- 1 cup water
- ½ cup reduced fat cream cheese, such as Neufchatel, softened
- ¼ cup light butter, softened
- 1 cup confectioners' sugar

Directions

1. Preheat the oven to 350 °F.

2. Butter and lightly flour a 9 x 13-inch baking pan.

3. Combine the pecans and coconut and sprinkle evenly over the bottom of the pan.

4. Prepare the cake mix batter using the yogurt and water in place of the recommended ingredients and pour over the coconut pecan mixture, spreading evenly.

Lightened up semi-homemade classics

5. In a medium bowl bean together the cream cheese, butter and confectioners' sugar until smooth. Drop heaped teaspoonfuls of the mixture onto the batter.

6. Bake until the cake is poofed and a toothpick inserted in the center comes out clean, about 45 minutes.

7. Cool cake completely in pan. To serve, cut a portion, scoop with a spatula and flip upside down onto a serving dish.

Information

Makes 18 servings
Each serving has 195 calories

83...Angel Food Lemon Icebox Cake

Low fat prepared angel food cake lends itself to easy semi-homemade creations that are both light and satisfying as in this classic style icebox cake.

Ingredients

- 1 (10-inch) ready-made angel food cake
- 1 (16 oz.) tub frozen light whipped topping, thawed
- 1 (3 oz.) box regular lemon gelatin

Directions

1. Using a long serrated bread knife, carefully slice the angel food cake into 3 layers. Place the bottom layer on a large cake plate, cut side up.

2. In a medium bowl, whisk together the whipped topping and the powdered gelatin until well combined.

3. Divide the topping into 4 parts and spread 1 part over the bottom layer. Place the second layer firmly on top and spread another portion of the topping over. Continue so that the final topping portion is used to ice the outside of the cake.

4. Refrigerate overnight until firm.

5. Slice with a serrated knife.

Lightened up semi-homemade classics

INFORMATION

Makes 10 servings
Each serving has 169 calories

84...Banana Split Icebox Cake

If banana splits are your yen, look no further than this easy reduced calorie cake that's deliciously creamy and satisfying.

Ingredients

- 1 (16 oz.) tub light whipped topping, thawed
- 1 cup nonfat plain Greek yogurt
- 1 small box instant sugar-free vanilla pudding
- 1 (8 oz.) can no-sugar-added crushed pineapple, drained
- 1 box low-fat graham crackers or reduced fat vanilla wafers
- 1 large banana, thinly sliced
- 1 cup chopped fresh strawberries
- Light chocolate sauce
- Maraschino cherries
- Chopped walnuts

Directions

1. In a large bowl mix together the whipped topping, yogurt, and vanilla pudding granules until well combined. Fold in the pineapple.

2. Line the bottom of a 9-inch square baking dish or casserole with one layer of grahams. Pour ¾ of the pudding mixture over and spread evenly. Place the banana slices evenly on top and sprinkle the strawberries over. Finish with another layer of the grahams and spread the remaining pudding mixture over.

Lightened up semi-homemade classics

3. Reserve remaining grahams for other purpose.
4. Cover with plastic wrap and refrigerate overnight.
5. Just before serving, drizzle the chocolate sauce over, place cherries on top, and sprinkle the nuts. Cut and serve.

Information

Makes 9 servings
Each serving has 200 calories

85... Oreo Cookie Lover's Icebox Cake

America's favorite cookie in reduced fat guise is crumbled and combined with pudding and Cool Whip for an Oreo showstopper of a dessert.

Ingredients

- 1 (15 oz.) package reduced fat Oreo cookies, crumbled
- ½ cup light butter, melted
- 1 (8 oz.) package reduced fat cream cheese such as Neufchatel, softened
- 1 cup confectioners' sugar
- 1 (12 oz.) tub light whipped topping, thawed
- 1 box sugar-free instant chocolate pudding

Directions

Set aside ½ cup of the crumbled Oreos.

In a medium bowl combine the remaining Oreos with the butter and press firmly into a 9 x 13-inch glass baking dish to form a bottom crust.

In another bowl beat together the cream cheese and sugar until light.

Scoop half the whipped topping into the bowl and stir in until well combined. Spoon over the prepared cookie crust and spread evenly. Chill for 30 minutes.

Meanwhile, make the chocolate pudding according to the package directions.

Lightened up semi-homemade classics

When the cream cheese layer is well chilled, spread the pudding mixture evenly over. Return to the refrigerator for at least one hour until set.

Spread the reserved whipped topping decoratively over the chilled pudding layer and sprinkle with the remaining crumbles cookies before serving.

Information

Makes 24 servings
Each serving has 198 calories

Pies and Fruit Desserts

86... Cheesecake Pie with Berry Glaze

A not-too-sweet chocolate wafer crust is the base for this reduced-fat creamy pie topped with a simple reduced sugar fruit glaze.

Ingredients

For crust

- 20 Nabisco chocolate wafers, crushed
- 2 level tbsp. light brown sugar
- 1 tbsp. unsalted butter, melted
- 1 large egg white, slightly beaten

For filling

- 1 cup low-fat cottage cheese, drained
- ½ cup reduced-fat cream cheese, such as Neufchatel
- 6 tbsp. granulated sugar
- 2 tbsp. all-purpose flour
- 1 tsp. vanilla
- 2 large eggs

For glaze

- 1 cup reduced-sugar strawberry jam
- ¼ cup hot water
- ½ cup diced strawberries

Pies and fruit desserts

DIRECTIONS

1. Preheat the oven to 350 °F. Coat a 9-inch pie pan with cooking spray.

2. In a medium bowl stir together the crust ingredients with a fork until well combined. Transfer to the pie pan and press evenly into the bottom and up the sides. Bake for 8 minutes.

3. In a food processor fitted with a steel blade process the cottage cheese, cream cheese, sugar, and flour until smooth. Add the vanilla and eggs and continue to process for 1 minute until well combined. Transfer to the baked pie crust and smooth over the top. Bake until just set, 30 to 35 minutes. Cool completely before proceeding with glaze. Chill in the fridge.

4. To make glaze whisk together the jam and hot water until smooth and no lumps appear. Stir in the diced strawberries. Spoon evenly over the chilled cheese filling and spread to the edges. Serve immediately or continue to chill until ready to serve.

INFORMATION

Makes 8 servings
Each serving has 198 calories

87...Creamy Key Lime Yogurt Pie

This easy no-bake treat makes use of rich and creamy Greek yogurt for a heavenly dessert that's amazingly low in fat and calories.

Ingredients

- 2 tbsp. cold water
- 1 tbsp. lime juice
- 1 ½ tsp. unflavored gelatin
- 3 (6 oz.) containers Key lime yogurt, such as Oikos
- ½ cup reduced-fat cream cheese, such as Neufchatel
- 1 tbsp. granulated sugar
- 1 tsp. grated lime zest
- ½ cup frozen light whipped topping, thawed
- 1 (8 or 9-inch) prepared reduced fat graham cracker crust

Directions

1. Combine water and lime juice in a small saucepan. Sprinkle gelatin over and let stand for 1 minute. Heat, stirring constantly, until gelatin is completely dissolved, about 2 minutes. Remove from heat and cool for 10 minutes.

2. Meanwhile in a medium bowl beat together the yogurt, cream cheese, sugar, and lime zest until smooth. Gently fold in whipped topping.

Pies and fruit desserts

3. Transfer to graham cracker crust and refrigerate until chilled and well set, 2 to 3 hours.

Information

Makes 8 servings
Each serving has 190 calories

88... Mixed Berry Tartlets

Any combination of seasonal berries will do in this delightfully fresh and low calorie treat that's perfect finished with a dollop of yogurt or whipped topping.

Ingredients

For filling

- ¼ cup granulated sugar
- 2 ½ tsp. (1 envelope) unflavored gelatin
- 1 (12 oz.) pkg. frozen mixed berries, thawed
- 1 lb. fresh mixed berries, trimmed if necessary, and diced

For crust

- 2/3 cup graham cracker crumbs
- 2 tbsp. granulated sugar
- 2 tbsp. unsalted butter, melted

Directions

1. Make filling first by combining all ingredients in a large saucepan. Cook over medium heat, stirring often, until gelatin is completely dissolved and mixture is bubbly. Transfer to a large bowl and refrigerate. Stir occasionally as mixture begins to set up, chilling for about 45 minutes.

2. Meanwhile coat a 9-inch square baking dish with cooking spray.

Pies and fruit desserts

3. Make the crust by combining the ingredients in a small bowl and stirring together with a fork until well combined. Transfer to the prepared pan and press evenly into the bottom only. When filling is ready, pour over the crust, spreading berries out evenly.

4. Refrigerate at least 3 hours or overnight before slicing and serving.

INFORMATION

Makes 9 servings
Each serving has 130 calories

89...Petite Pecan Pies

These single serve pies feature all the great flavor and consistency of classic Southern pecan pies without the extra sugar and calories.

Ingredients

For crust

- ½ cup reduced-fat cream cheese, such as Neufchatel
- ¼ cup light buttery spread, such as Earth Balance
- 1 cup all-purpose flour

For filling

- 2 large eggs
- 1/3 cup granulated sugar
- ¼ cup pure maple syrup
- ½ tsp. vanilla
- 1 tbsp. unsalted butter, melted
- ¾ cup chopped pecans

Directions

1. Preheat the oven to 325 °F.
2. Prepare crust by combining all ingredients in a food processor and pulsing until smooth. Gather dough and divide into 12 equal portions. Press each portion evenly into ungreased standard muffin tin cups, in bottom and up sides. Bake for 12 minutes and set aside.

Pies and fruit desserts

3. Make filling by beating together eggs, sugar, maple syrup, and vanilla in a medium bowl until well combined. Beat in melted butter. Stir in pecans.

4. Evenly divide filling between the 12 muffin cup crusts and bake until crust is browned and the filling has puffed up. Transfer muffin tin to a wire rack to cool completely, or serve warm.

INFORMATION

Makes 12 servings
Each serving has 175 calories

90...Florida Cobbler

The fresh flavor of Florida citrus is featured in this unusual cobbler that's delicious topped with a spoonful of vanilla Greek style yogurt.

Ingredients

For filling

- 6 medium navel oranges, peeled, seeded and sectioned
- 2 pink or red grapefruit, peeled, seeded and sectioned
- ¼ cup water
- 3 tbsp. granulated sugar
- 1 tbsp. cornstarch
- Dash ground ginger

For topping

- 1 cup all-purpose flour
- 1 tbsp. granulated sugar
- 1 ½ tsp. baking powder
- 1/8 tsp. salt
- Dash ground nutmeg
- 2 tbsp. unsalted butter, diced
- 1 large egg
- 1 tbsp. low-fat milk
- 1/3 cup plain low-fat yogurt
- 2 tbsp. flaked coconut
- Vanilla Greek yogurt for serving

Pies and fruit desserts

DIRECTIONS

1. Preheat the oven to 375 °F. Lightly coat a 2-quart baking dish with cooking spray.

2. In a large saucepan combine all the filling ingredients and bring to a simmer over medium heat. Stir often, allowing to thicken, about 3 minutes. Set aside.

3. Make the cobbler topping: Whisk together the flour, sugar, baking powder, salt and nutmeg. Add the diced butter and work with a pastry blender or fork until crumb-like. In another bowl whisk together the egg, milk, and yogurt. Add the wet mixture to the dry and mix just to combine. Stir in the coconut.

4. Pour the filling into the prepared dish. Drop spoonfuls of the cobbler dough over the top to make 9 mounds. Bake until the filling is bubbly and a toothpick inserted in the cobbler comes out clean, 20 to 25 minutes.

5. Cool slightly before serving, topped with yogurt.

INFORMATION

Makes 9 servings
Each serving has 190 calories

91...Easy Blackberry and Peach Crisp

Delicious fresh fruit highlights this super quick dessert that's made on top of the stove and topped with the crunch of pecans and toasted oats.

Ingredients

- 2 tbsp. light butter
- ¼ cup chopped pecans
- ¼ cup old fashioned rolled oats
- 2 tbsp. flaked coconut
- 1 heaping tbsp. light brown sugar
- Dash ground cinnamon
- 4 medium peaches, pitted and sliced
- 1 tbsp. lemon juice
- 2 tsp. granulated sugar
- 1 cup fresh blackberries
- Dollop light whipped topping

Directions

1. Melt half the butter in a large nonstick skillet over medium heat. Add the pecans, oats, coconut, brown sugar, and cinnamon and cook, stirring often, until lightly toasted and brown, about 5 minutes. Transfer to a sheet of parchment paper and set aside.

2. Wipe out skillet and melt remaining butter over medium heat. Add the peaches, lemon juice and sugar and stir well. Cook until bubbly, stirring often and well heated through, 3 to 5 minutes. Fold in the blackberries.

3. To serve, spoon the fruit into a serving dish, top with some of the oat crunch, and add a dollop of whipped topping.

INFORMATION

Makes 6 servings
Each serving has 198 calories

92...Baked Berry Crisp

Frozen bags of mixed berries make this a snap to prepare and are great to have on hand when fresh are less than peak in flavor.

Ingredients

- 1 (16 oz.) bag frozen mixed berries, no-sugar-added
- 1 tbsp. all-purpose flour
- 2 tbsp. granulated sugar
- 1 cup low fat granola cereal

Directions

1. Preheat the oven to 375 °F.
2. Place the frozen berries in an 8-inch round baking dish and sprinkle with the flour and sugar. Toss gently to coat.
3. Bake berries for 20 minutes and stir gently. Top with the granola and return to the oven.
4. Bake until the berries are bubbly and the granola is crisp and golden, about 15 minutes more.
5. Serve warm.

Information

Makes 6 servings
Each serving has 130 calories

Pies and fruit desserts

93... Phyllo Apple Strudel

Thin sheets of Greek-style pastry are ideal for this lighter version of an Austrian classic with the great flavor of cinnamon and nutmeg.

Ingredients

- 4 large apples, such as Golden Delicious, peeled, cored and chopped
- 2 tbsp. packed light brown sugar
- 2 tbsp. currants or raisins
- 2 tbsp. chopped walnuts
- 1 tbsp. apple brandy or cider
- ½ tsp. ground cinnamon
- ¼ tsp. ground nutmeg
- 6 sheets (14 x 9-inches) frozen phyllo dough, thawed
- Butter flavored cooking spray

Directions

1. Preheat the oven to 350 °F. Line a rimmed baking sheet with parchment paper.

2. In a large bowl toss together all the ingredients except the phyllo and spray until well combined.

3. Lightly coat the parchment paper with cooking spray. Place 1 sheet of phyllo on top. Coat lightly with cooking spray and place another sheet of phyllo on top. Repeat with all 6 sheets.

4. Spread the apple filling over the phyllo leaving 1 inch uncovered on all sides. Roll up from the long end, folding in the sides halfway, and continuing to roll into a long cigar shape.

5. Place seam side down and spray again on top.

6. Bake until crisp and golden, about 45 minutes.

7. Transfer with parchment to a wire rack to cool before slicing.

Information

Makes 6 servings
Each serving has 135 calories

94...Phyllo Fruit Napoleons

A light cheese filling and crisp layers of phyllo pastry highlight this delectable dessert that can be made with any type of fruit in season.

Ingredients

- 9 sheets (14 x 9-inches) frozen phyllo dough, thawed
- Butter flavored cooking spray
- Confectioners' sugar for dusting
- 3 cups fresh diced fruit such as kiwi, grapes, melon and mango
- 2 tsp. granulated sugar
- 2 tsp. lemon juice
- 1 oz. plain goat cheese, softened
- 1 (3 oz.) pkg. reduced fat cream cheese
- 1 tbsp. honey

Directions

1. Preheat the oven to 350 °F. Line a baking sheet with parchment paper.

2. Place 1 sheet of phyllo on a flat work surface, coat lightly with cooking spray and dust with the sugar. Repeat with remaining sheets. Cut into 6 squares and place on the prepared baking sheet an inch apart.

3. Bake until crisp and puffed, about 10 minutes. Set aside to cool.

Pies and fruit desserts

4. Meanwhile in a medium bowl toss together the fruit with the sugar and lemon juice. In another bowl stir together the cheeses and honey.

5. To assemble, take 1 puffed phyllo square and using a sharp knife, cut sideways into 3 squares. Place bottom square on a serving plate, top with some of the cheese mixture and fruit and continue with the next layer, finishing with the 3rd square.

6. Dust with confectioners' sugar and serve.

INFORMATION

Makes 6 servings
Each serving has 185 calories

95...Dessert Nachos with Chocolate Drizzle

Finish off a Mexican themed dinner with this delightfully sweet rendition of a popular appetizer made with succulent raspberries and healthy yogurt.

Ingredients

- 2 (8-inch) whole grain tortillas
- 2 tsp. unsalted butter, melted
- 2 tsp. cinnamon sugar
- 1 cup low-fat vanilla Greek yogurt
- 1 cup fresh raspberries
- 2 tbsp. light chocolate syrup
- 2 tsp. sliced almonds

Directions

1. Preheat the oven to 400 °F. Line a rimmed baking sheet with parchment paper.

2. Brush each tortilla with the melted butter and cut into 6 triangles each. Transfer in a single layer to the prepared baking sheet and sprinkle with the cinnamon sugar.

3. Bake the tortilla chips until lightly golden and crispy, about 8 minutes and set aside to cool.

4. When ready to serve, arrange 6 tortilla chips on a serving plate and dollop half the yogurt over. Sprinkle half the berries over, drizzle 1 tbsp. of chocolate syrup decoratively, and top with half the almonds.

5. Repeat for the second serving.

Information

Makes 2 servings
Each serving has 197 calories

96...Better-For-You Strawberry Shortcakes

These fiber-rich, lower fat shortcakes with a yogurt fillings and fresh strawberries will become a true summer favorite.

Ingredients

For the cakes

- 1 ¼ cups all-purpose flour
- ¾ cup old fashioned oats
- 1 ½ tsp. baking powder
- ½ tsp. baking soda
- ¼ tsp. salt
- 3 tbsp. granulated sugar
- 2 tbsp. light butter, diced
- ¾ cup low-fat buttermilk
- 1 large egg white

To serve

- 2 lb. fresh strawberries, hulled and sliced
- 2 tbsp. granulated sugar
- 1 ½ cups plain non-fat Greek yogurt
- Honey for drizzling

Pies and fruit desserts

Directions

1. Preheat the oven 425 °F. Line a cookie sheet with parchment paper.

2. Place the flour and oats in a food processor and pulse until the oats have ground fine. Add the baking powder, baking soda, salt, and sugar and pulse 2 more times. Add the butter and pulse until mixture appears crumbly. Add buttermilk and egg white and pulse until just combined.

3. Drop by spoonfuls onto the prepared cookie sheet to make 8 shortcakes. Shape evenly with a fork and bake until lightly golden on top and a toothpick inserted in the center comes out clean, about 15 minutes. Transfer shortcakes to a wire rack to cool.

4. In a large bowl toss together the sliced strawberries and set aside for at least 15 minutes, occasionally stirring.

5. When ready to serve, slice the shortcakes in half and place the bottoms on serving plates. Top with a generous portion of the strawberries and add 2 heaping spoonfuls of yogurt.

6. Drizzle with a little honey and top with the other half of the shortcake. Serve immediately.

Information

Makes 8 servings
Each serving has 189 calories

97... GINGER SHORTCAKES WITH BLUEBERRIES

Crystallized ginger jazzes up these delicious low fat cakes topped with a lemony filling and fresh blueberries.

INGREDIENTS

For the cakes

- 1 cup all-purpose flour
- 2 tbsp. packed light brown sugar
- 1 tsp. baking powder
- 1/8 tsp. baking soda
- 2 tbsp. light butter, diced
- ½ cup low-fat buttermilk
- 1 ½ tbsp. chopped crystallized ginger

To serve

- 1 cup lemon flavored low-fat yogurt
- 1 ½ cups fresh blueberries
- Dollop light whipped topping

DIRECTIONS

1. Preheat the oven 425 °F. Line a cookie sheet with parchment paper.

2. In a medium bowl whisk together the flour, brown sugar, baking powder, and baking soda. Add the diced butter and use a pastry blender or fork to work the mixture until crumbly. Stir in the buttermilk and ginger just to combine.

3. Drop rounded spoonfuls of the mixture onto the prepared cookie sheet to make 6 shortcakes. Evenly shape with a fork and bake until lightly golden and a toothpick inserted in the center comes out clean, about 12 minutes. Transfer to a wire rack to cool.

4. To serve, slice the shortcakes in half and place the bottoms on serving plates. Place 2 heaping spoonfuls of the lemon yogurt over the bottom and sprinkle blueberries over. Top with the other half of the shortcake and a dollop of whipped topping.

INFORMATION

Makes 6 servings
Each serving has 172 calories

98...Individual Orange White Chocolate Trifles

Purchased lady fingers make this easy to create while a reduced calorie pudding mix cuts back on the guilt but not the flavor.

Ingredients

- 2 cups low-fat milk
- 1 pkg. white chocolate reduced calorie pudding mix
- 6 mandarin or Clementine oranges, peeled and segmented
- ¼ cup orange juice
- 1/8 tsp. orange blossom water
- 24 soft lady fingers
- 6 tbsp. light whipped topping
- Grated white chocolate (optional)

Directions

1. Using the low-fat milk prepare the white chocolate pudding according to package directions and chill slightly. Have ready the segmented oranges, a bowl with the orange juice and orange blossom water combined, and 6 parfait or dessert glasses.

2. Use 2 lady fingers for covering the bottom of each parfait glass. Brush them lightly with the orange juice mixture and top with a little of the pudding. Place a few orange segments on top and repeat with the remaining lady fingers. Finish each with a tbsp. of light whipped topping spread to cover. Top with a little grated chocolate if desired.

3. Refrigerate for at least 1 hour before serving.

Information

Makes 6 servings
Each serving has 185 calories

99...Dressed Up Fruit Salad

A simple bowl of fresh fruit becomes a gourmet treat in this easy-to-make rendition that features fresh mint, honey and a bit of creamy luxury when nothing else will do.

Ingredients

- 2 cups assorted fresh fruit cut into bite-size pieces
- 1 tbsp. chopped fresh mint leaves
- 1 tbsp. lime juice
- 1 tbsp. orange juice
- 1 tbsp. honey
- ¼ cup whipping cream

Directions

1. Place cut fruit in a medium bowl. In another bowl whisk together the mint, lime juice, orange juice and honey. Pour over the fruit, toss gently to coat and refrigerate until ready to serve.

2. Just before serving place the cream in a chilled medium bowl and using a whisk, lightly beat until just beginning to thicken but no peaks have formed.

3. Spoon the fruit mixture into serving bowls and pour the thickened cream over.

INFORMATION

Makes 2 servings
Each serving has 189 calories

100...Healthy Style Fruit Ambrosia

Delicious and thick Greek yogurt steps in for the sour cream and heavy cream in this healthier version that you'll love diving into.

Ingredients

   2 cups diced fresh pineapple
   2 medium peaches, pitted and diced
   1 cup fresh cherries, halved and pitted
   1 cup low-fat vanilla Greek yogurt
   2 tbsp. reduced-sugar apricot jam or spread
   ¼ cup mini marshmallows
   1 tbsp. flaked coconut
   1 tbsp. chopped pecans

Directions

1. In a large bowl combine the pineapple, peaches, and cherries.

2. In another bowl whisk together the yogurt and apricot jam.

3. Fold the yogurt mixture into the fruit mixture and refrigerate for at least 1 hour.

4. To serve, stir the fruit well and divide between 4 serving dishes. Sprinkle each with the marshmallows, coconut and pecans just before serving.

Pies and fruit desserts

INFORMATION

Makes 4 servings
Each serving has 165 calories

Temperature and Weight Conversion Charts

Weights

½ oz	10g
¾ oz	20g
1 oz	25g
1½ oz	40g
2 oz	50g
2½ oz	60g
3 oz	75g
4 oz	110g
4½ oz	125g
5 oz	150g
6 oz	175g
7 oz	200g
8 oz	225g
9 oz	250g
10 oz	275g
12 oz	350g
1 lb	450g
2 lb	900g
3 lb	1350g

Liquid Measures

1 tbsp	½ fl. oz	15ml
1/8 cup	1 fl. oz	30ml
¼ cup	2 fl. oz	60ml
½ cup	4 fl. oz	120ml
1 cup	8 fl. oz	240ml
1 pint	16 fl. oz	480ml

Temperatures

°F	°C	Gas Mark
275°F	140°C	1
300°F	150°C	2
325°F	170°C	3
350°F	180°C	4
375°F	190°C	5
400°F	200°C	6
425°F	210°C	7
450°F	220°C	8
475°F	230°C	9

American Cup Measures

1 cup flour	5oz	150g
1 cup caster/ granulated sugar	8oz	225g
1 cup brown sugar	6oz	175g
1 cup butter/margarine/lard	8oz	225g
1 cup sultanas/raisins	7oz	200g
1 cup currants	5oz	150g
1 cup ground almonds	4oz	110g
1 cup golden syrup	12oz	350g
1 cup uncooked rice	7oz	200g
1 cup grated cheese	4oz	110g
1 stick butter	4oz	110g

Glossary and Substitutions

Agave syrup
Use honey or maple syrup instead.

All-purpose Flour
Plain Flour.

Angel Food Cake Mix
Use a standard sponge cake mix (e.g. Victoria Sponge mix).

Angel Food Cake (ready made)
Use a plain sponge cake or a Madeira cake.

Baking Soda
Bicarbonate of Soda.

Buttermilk (low fat)
This can usually be found in stores, but you can make your own. To make 1 cup, mix 1 tbsp. vinegar or lemon juice with enough skimmed (fat-free) milk to make up to 1 cup.

Cake Flour
A soft flour such as McDougall's Supreme Sponge Flour. If that is not available then you can make your own:
- 1 cup cake flour = ¾ cup (105g) of plain flour mixed with 3 tbsp. cornflour.
- Cake Mixes (Vanilla/White/Yellow)
- Use Betty Crocker UK Classic Vanilla.
- Confectioners' Sugar
- Icing Sugar
- Corn Starch
- Cornflour

Dark Chocolate Kisses

Hershey's kisses can be ordered from http://bit.ly/16ZCmpG or http://bit.ly/cdGqL6

Flaked Coconut

Desiccated coconut, you can also use this for shredded coconut.

German Chocolate Cake Mix

Betty Crocker makes a German Chocolate Cake Mix which can be ordered from Amazon UK but if it is not available, a good substitute would be Betty Crocker UK Milk Chocolate Layer Cake Mix.

Graham Crackers

In the UK these are called digestive biscuits. McVities make light versions of their plain digestives and the chocolate ones.

Grape Drink Mix

Kool-Aid Unsweetened Grape Drink Mix can be ordered at Amazon UK, http://bit.ly/16ZCmpG or http://bit.ly/cdGqL6. Alternatively, you could use Ribena Light Concentrate.

Half and Half (low-fat)

Use light single cream such as Elmlea Single Light Cream.

Lady Fingers

Trifle sponge fingers

Light Biscuit Mix

Use a light scone mix (following recipe to make drop scones). If you can't find a light mix then add 10-15 calories per serving.

Molasses

If you can't find molasses, you can use black treacle.

Nasbico Chocolate Wafers

There isn't a European version of these but you can buy Necco's version at http://bit.ly/1bieKQn or there is a recipe at http://bit.ly/12xZBU4

Neufchatel Reduced-fat cream cheese

Use Philadelphia Light or store's own brand light cream cheese.

Old-fashioned Oats

Rolled Oats.

Orange Blossom Water

Orange Flower Water. If it's unavailable, try ½ tsp. orange extract and 1 tsp. lemon juice.

Phyllo Pastry

In the UK, this is called Filo pastry.

PKG

Abbreviation of Package.

Pudding mixes

For the vanilla, substitute Bird's Low Fat Instant Custard. For the chocolate, substitute Reduced Sugar Angel Delight (chocolate flavor). For white chocolate you could substitute with either Reduced Sugar Angel Delight (vanilla flavor) or for a twist the Reduced Sugar Angel Delight (strawberry flavor).

Pumpkin Pie Spice

Mix 4 tbsp. ground cinnamon, 4 tsp. nutmeg, 4 tsp. ground ginger and 3 tsp. ground allspice, and keep in an airtight spice jar.

Pumpkin Puree

If you can't find this in stores, you can make your own. See http://bit.ly/3YmRZ3 for a recipe.

ISBN-10: 1482055015
ISBN-13: 978-1482055016

Join Beth on her journey to lose weight and gain a new healthy life with this revolutionary new take on dieting. Beth describes "the simple way to health and weight-loss" where you can lose weight without denying yourself life's pleasures, lose fat while retaining lean mass and decrease your risk of obesity-related disorders.

This book outlines an easy to follow plan which will quickly become a habit just like it has for Beth and her husband, along with many thousands of other people.

Finally you can enjoy your food without feeling guilty!

ISBN-10: 1482005050
ISBN-13: 978-1482005059

Looking for delicious and healthy meals which will fit perfectly into any diet? Look no further than "100 Under 500 Calorie Meals", the ideal complement to "100 Under 200 Calorie Desserts" and "Easy Alternate Day Fasting".

Beth covers starters, sides, poultry, salads, soups, fish, meat and even Christmas and Thanksgiving meals with her simple to follow and delicious recipes. And for all the dessert lovers out there, there are yet more amazing recipes for you too!

Together with Beth, you're on your way to a fitter healthier life!

Other Books from MadeGlobal Publishing

- 100 Under 500 Calorie Meals - Beth Christian
- Easy Alternate Day Fasting - Beth Christian
- 100 Under 200 Calorie Desserts - Beth Christian
- The Fall of Anne Boleyn - Claire Ridgway
- The Anne Boleyn Collection - Claire Ridgway
- On This Day in Tudor History - Claire Ridgway
- Interviews with Indie Authors - Claire Ridgway
- The Merry Wives of Henry VIII - Ann Nonny
- Popular - Gareth Russell
- The Immaculate Deception - Gareth Russell
- Talia's Adventures - Verity Ridgway
- Las Aventuras de Talia (Spanish) - Verity Ridgway
- A Mountain Road - Douglas Weddell Thompson

Please Leave a Review

If you enjoyed this book, please leave a review on Amazon or at the book seller where you purchased it. There is no better way to thank the author and it really does make a huge difference! Thank you in advance.

Visit the Website for the Book:

http://www.easyalternatedayfasting.com/

You'll find tips, ideas and more things to help you achieve the life you want. Beth looks forward to seeing you there.

PRAISE FOR BOOKS BY BETH CHRISTIAN

100 UNDER 500 CALORIE MEALS

The recipes look delicious and easy ... it is very user friendly and breaks down the calorie count for the recipes.
Sweetea

I'm always looking for good, clean, healthy recipes, and this book has plenty. Not too many ingredients, not too much chopping or mixing, but tasty and nutritious.
M. *Thomson*

I'm always looking for good, clean, healthy recipes, and this book has plenty. Not too many ingredients, not too much chopping or mixing, but tasty and nutritious.
"Susie's mom"

Quick and easy to make healthy meals.
Sherry Brossett

ON EASY ALTERNATE DAY FASTING

I love a book that just gives you the information you need and nothing more. This great book was to-the-point with no "skimming" material. So much great and easy to understand information.
Jean Barber

This diet makes sense! Easy and no brainer.
S. Williams

Just completed first week following guidelines from "The Easy Alternate day Fasting" & so amazed at results - best diet book I have purchased!
Maria

Printed in Great Britain
by Amazon.co.uk, Ltd.,
Marston Gate.